Drupal 7 Views Cookbook

Over 50 recipes to master the creation of views using the Drupal Views 3 module

J. Ayen Green

BIRMINGHAM - MUMBAI

Drupal 7 Views Cookbook

First published: March 2012

Production Reference: 2230312

Published by Packt Publishing Ltd.
Livery Place
35 Livery Street
Birmingham B3 2PB, UK.

ISBN 978-1-84951-434-7

www.packtpub.com

Cover Image by Duraid Fatouhi (duraidfatouhi@yahoo.com)

Credits

Author

J. Ayen Green

Reviewers

Dave Hall

Dlair Kadhem

Deepak Vohra

Acquisition Editor

Usha Iyer

Lead Technical Editor

Meeta Rajani

Technical Editors

Mehreen Shaikh

Azharuddin Sheikh

Copy Editors

Leonard D'Silva

Aaron Rosario

Neha Shetty

Project Coordinator

Shubhanjan Chatterjee

Proofreader

Aaron Nash

Indexer

Monica Ajmera Mehta

Production Coordinator

Melwyn D'sa

Cover Work

Melwyn D'sa

About the Author

J. Ayen Green (`@accidentalcoder`, `theAccidentalCoder.com`) has developed software since inventing the abacus, created websites since [insert name du jour] created the Web, and has been a Drupaler somewhat longer than his current D.O. UID (try settling on an ID when your real name is Dries Webchick). He is a writer and columnist of sorts, a poet of metered sorts, husband, father, friend, and a rascal (in the nicest possible way). When not plugged in, Green enjoys nature, dogs, horses, and other critters, riding his Harley, kayaking, spicy food, the arts, and other cultures. He and his wife, Sofía-Aileen, reside in New York City.

This was my third title for Packt, yet was a unique experience. If I may be allowed to make a resolution outside of New Year's, it is to never start a book about software that is alpha (as were both Drupal 7 and Views 3 during my first draft) or undergoing a UI change (as was Views 3 during my second draft, which, out of necessity, then became a new first draft). Despite the pitfalls, I had unending support from my publisher. I thank those responsible for a ride smoother than it might have been: Chaitanya Apte , Meeta Rajani, Mehreen Shaikh, and Neha Mallik, and the rest of the editorial staff, Rebecca Sawant and Shubhanjan Chatterjee, project coordinators, and all those who will have provided the production services after this Acknowledgment was written.

My technical reviewers showed patience and endurance beyond the normal call of duty.

My wife, Sofia-Aileen, weathered this project and my curmudgeon-like orneriness with cheery aplomb. Thanks for knowing what I need before I do.

My thanks to Dries Buytaert for Drupal, to Angie Byron for getting Drupal 7 out the door as quickly and as humanly possible, and especially a hardy thank you to Earl Miles, a.k.a merlinofchaos, for Views and his kind and patient assistance for the several times I was at wit's end, as well as the team that brought the new UI to life.

About the Reviewers

Dave Hall has worked as an open source consultant and advocate, specializing in web applications, for over a decade. He is currently working as an Architect and Lead Developer for enterprise clients pushing the boundaries of what is possible with Drupal.

Dave has a keen interest in performance, scalability, and security. In 2009, he designed, deployed, and maintained more than 2000 production Drupal 6 sites for a single client.

Dave has contributed to numerous open source projects, including Drupal core, phpGroupWare, StatusNet, and PEAR.

Dlair Kadhem immigrated to the United Kingdom in 1996 having fled war-torn Iraq to seek a better life. In 2005, he went on to graduate with a degree in Electronics Systems Engineering from the University of Essex. Upon completing his degree, he decided to further explore the world of computing, specializing in online services and web applications.

Dlair always had a fascination for creativity and technology. He first encountered computers in 1997 at the age of 13. In the following year, he launched his first website using free web space provided by Freeserve and went on to create ground-breaking online communities.

Dlair spent the early part of his career working in web design, online marketing, and software development. Having gained valuable industry experience, Dlair founded his own business in 2006 with the clear vision of bringing people and technology together through innovation and open source technology. Some of his clients include the BBC, Bauer Publishing, Croydon Council, Department of Health, Harrods, London College of Communication, NHS, and Red Bee Media.

With a keen interest in the evolution of technology, Dlair is currently focused on the rapid innovation taking place in the world of handheld devices and how they affect everyday life. His goal is to build a revolutionary business to create and develop products and services that will increase people's quality of living.

Deepak Vohra is a consultant and a principal member of the NuBean.com software company. Deepak is a Sun Certified Java Programmer and Web Component Developer, and has worked in the fields of XML and Java programming and J2EE for over five years. Deepak is the co-author of the *Apress* book *Pro XML Development with Java Technology* and was the technical reviewer for the *O'Reilly* book *WebLogic: The Definitive Guide*. Deepak was also the technical reviewer for the *Course Technology PTR* book *Ruby Programming for the Absolute Beginner,* and the technical editor for the *Manning Publications* book *Prototype and Scriptaculous in Action*. Deepak is also the author of the *Packt Publishing* books *JDBC 4.0 and Oracle JDeveloper for J2EE Development, Processing XML Documents with Oracle JDeveloper 11g,* and *EJB 3.0 Database Persistence with Oracle Fusion Middleware 11g*.

www.PacktPub.com

Support files, eBooks, discount offers and more

You might want to visit www.PacktPub.com for support files and downloads related to your book.

Did you know that Packt offers eBook versions of every book published, with PDF and ePub files available? You can upgrade to the eBook version at www.PacktPub.com and as a print book customer, you are entitled to a discount on the eBook copy. Get in touch with us at service@packtpub.com for more details.

At www.PacktPub.com, you can also read a collection of free technical articles, sign up for a range of free newsletters and receive exclusive discounts and offers on Packt books and eBooks.

http://PacktLib.PacktPub.com

Do you need instant solutions to your IT questions? PacktLib is Packt's online digital book library. Here, you can access, read and search across Packt's entire library of books.

Why Subscribe?

- ▶ Fully searchable across every book published by Packt
- ▶ Copy and paste, print and bookmark content
- ▶ On demand and accessible via web browser

Free Access for Packt account holders

If you have an account with Packt at www.PacktPub.com, you can use this to access PacktLib today and view nine entirely free books. Simply use your login credentials for immediate access.

This book is dedicated to my children, who will never read it, but will think it's cool, nonetheless.

Table of Contents

Preface

Views is a contributed module that was originally written by Earl Miles, who is known as merlinofchaos, or simply Merlin in the Drupal community. The module is maintained by him and others in the Drupal community.

Views 1 was written during the Summer of Code in 2005, and was available for Drupal 4.6, 4.7, and for Drupal 5 in 2006. For those still running a Drupal 5 site, there is a Drupal 5 *Views Recipes* book from Packt Publishing.

Views 2 was first released in 2008 for Drupal 6, and was a major improvement on an already very useful module. There isn't a book with recipes on Views 2, but you can find many good examples of using Views 2 in Drupal 6 Attachment Views from Packt Publishing.

Views 3 for Drupal 7 is still in beta as I write this introduction, but will be released before I get to the appendix!

What is a view?

From a general perspective: You must have just installed Drupal and the default website it creates. You have also added a few articles and assigned a descriptive term to each, that is, a category. Now, you would like to present the visitors with a page containing articles of a specific category. How do you do it? The short answer is...you can't...yet.

Alright, you decide to put that idea aside for now, and instead present all articles, but sorted by their titles. How do you do it? The short answer, again, is...you can't...yet.

The fact is that of the laundry list of thousands of functions available with Drupal, painstaking thoughts go into deciding which of them will be present "in core", that is, in the code when first installed, before anything else is added. Generally, the philosophy is that only the mission-critical functions should be present. Keeping the base platform light and fast is preferable to bloating it with functionality that can, instead, be added via contributed modules. Enter Views.

We will be exploring the capabilities of the Views module throughout the book, so for now, here is a short, in-a-nutshell definition of what this module offers.

 The Views module provides the capability, via a program code or the included user interface submodule, to define the criteria by which to select content, process it, manipulate it, and format its presentation. It is, at its heart, a query generator with many additional functional layers.

Many would say that a fully functional Drupal site would be almost impossible to produce without the use of the Views module, and I agree. Now, do not take that as a challenge. Of course it would be possible to write custom modules in order to purposely accomplish a rich site without using the Views module, but why bother?

From a MySQL perspective: If you are not familiar with MySQL, it stands for My Structured Query Language and is the most used database with Drupal. The database contains Drupal's settings as well as the content added to the website.

So, let us say that we have a table in our database, and it is called `node`, and in this table we keep whatever content we have added to the website. If we want to retrieve all the content from this table, the command given to MySQL would be:

```
SELECT * FROM node;
```

This would return all the data stored in that table, each piece of content being a row (a record). If we wanted to retrieve only `blog` content, the command would be:

```
SELECT * FROM node WHERE node_type='blog';
```

If we want to sort the records by the title of the `blog` entries:

```
SELECT * FROM node WHERE node_type='blog' ORDER BY title;
```

Specifying that only three records are desired would be:

```
SELECT * FROM node WHERE node_type='blog' ORDER BY title LIMIT 0,3;
```

Finally, if there was another table, `blog-topic`, this table uses the same identifying value as the node table, `nid` (such as a driver's license number), and if we want to return its data along with the node data, we would relate the two records to each other, shown as follows:

```
SELECT * FROM node JOIN blog-topic ON node.nid=blog-topic.nid WHERE
node_type='blog' ORDER BY title LIMIT 0,3;
```

Views does all that for you, as well as gives you many options to format its output to suit your needs.

 The term View comes up in other places in computing, such as with SQL, but in the context of Drupal, it almost always refers to a dynamic display created with the Views module.

Views is a particularly versatile module, in terms of interactions with the developer, who will use it in any or all of the following three ways:

- Via the UI (user interface) for creating views that are editable by the admin or other authorized users
- From within a custom module, creating and/or invoking a view programmatically
- Indirectly, using modules that themselves create programmatic views

Views offers many of the tools necessary for meeting your needs:

- Template hints and model templates
- Several types of default views
- Various display types to meet the needs of the layout such as page, block, and attachment
- A number of output formats such as tabular, grid, and list
- Hooks
- Pluggable features such as handlers and formatters
- Instantaneous AJAX previewing

It is no wonder that Views is consistently the most popularly downloaded module at `Drupal.org`!

What this book covers

Chapter 1, Modifying Default Views, gives an introduction to the Views UI by modifying *some of the* views that come with the module in order to make useful versions of them.

Chapter 2, Basic Custom Views, covers creating elementary views and how to get them to provide the information you need.

Chapter 3, Intermediate Custom Views, goes beyond the basics to introduce concepts such as presenting teasers for a specific type of content, adding a header and footer, using AJAX for page changes, and producing custom links.

Chapter 4, Creating Advanced Views, covers advanced topics such as the use of multiple displays, using dynamic filters with depth, and restricting access to Views.

Chapter 5, Intermediate Custom Theming Views, shows you the various ways to manipulate the output of a view so that it has the look that you need.

Chapter 6, Creating Views Programmatically, shows how to create a view from within the module code rather than using the UI.

Chapter 7, Views Administration, covers some of the tools for administering your Views environment.

Appendix A, Installing Views, provides instructions for installing the Views module.

Appendix B, Entity Types and Fields, gives instructions for creating the various content types and other Drupal elements used in the recipes.

What you need for this book

You will need a reasonably advanced computer and an Internet connection. All software required to do the recipes can be freely obtained from `drupal.org`.

Who this book is for

This book is for developers or technically proficient users who are fairly comfortable with the concepts behind websites and the Drupal environment.

Conventions

In this book, you will find a number of styles of text that distinguish between different kinds of information. Here are some examples of these styles, and an explanation of their meaning.

Code words in text are shown as follows: "However, we do not want to use that argument, because we will not be retrieving content based on the `nid` in the attachment, we will be retrieving content based on `tid`."

A block of code is set as follows:

```
<style type="text/css">
#cc-container {
  width: 180px;
}
.cc-odd, .cc-even {
  padding: 6px;
  border: 4px solid black;
  width: 120px;
  position: relative;
  text-align: center;
}
.cc-odd {
  left: 0;
```

```
    background-color: #aaa;
  }
  .cc-even {
    left: 60px;
    background-color: #eee;
  }
  .cc-value {
    font-size: 36px;
  }
  </style>
```

When we wish to draw your attention to a particular part of a code block, the relevant lines or items are set in bold:

```
<?php foreach ($rows as $id => $row): ?>
  <div class="cc-<?php echo ($ctr % 2) ? 'odd' : 'even'; ?>">
    <?php $ctr--; ?>
    <div class="cc-value"><?php echo $ctr; ?></div>
    <div class="<?php print $classes_array[$id]; ?>">
      <?php print $row; ?>
    </div>
  </div>
<?php endforeach; ?>
```

New terms and **important words** are shown in bold. Words that you see on the screen, in menus or dialog boxes for example, appear in the text like this: " Click on the **Title** link in the **Title** box and change the title to **Recent article comments**, and then click on the **Update** button."

 Warnings or important notes appear in a box like this.

 Tips and tricks appear like this.

Reader feedback

Feedback from our readers is always welcome. Let us know what you think about this book—what you liked or may have disliked. Reader feedback is important for us to develop titles that you really get the most out of.

To send us general feedback, simply send an e-mail to feedback@packtpub.com, and mention the book title through the subject of your message.

If there is a topic that you have expertise in and you are interested in either writing or contributing to a book, see our author guide on www.packtpub.com/authors.

Customer support

Now that you are the proud owner of a Packt book, we have a number of things to help you to get the most from your purchase.

Downloading the example code

You can download the example code files for all Packt books you have purchased from your account at http://www.packtpub.com. If you purchased this book elsewhere, you can visit http://www.packtpub.com/support and register to have the files e-mailed directly to you.

Errata

Although we have taken every care to ensure the accuracy of our content, mistakes do happen. If you find a mistake in one of our books—maybe a mistake in the text or the code—we would be grateful if you would report this to us. By doing so, you can save other readers from frustration and help us improve subsequent versions of this book. If you find any errata, please report them by visiting http://www.packtpub.com/support, selecting your book, clicking on the **errata submission form** link, and entering the details of your errata. Once your errata are verified, your submission will be accepted and the errata will be uploaded to our website, or added to any list of existing errata, under the Errata section of that title.

Piracy

Piracy of copyright material on the Internet is an ongoing problem across all media. At Packt, we take the protection of our copyright and licenses very seriously. If you come across any illegal copies of our works, in any form, on the Internet, please provide us with the location address or website name immediately so that we can pursue a remedy.

Please contact us at copyright@packtpub.com with a link to the suspected pirated material.

We appreciate your help in protecting our authors, and our ability to bring you valuable content.

Questions

You can contact us at questions@packtpub.com if you are having a problem with any aspect of the book, and we will do our best to address it.

1
Modifying Default Views

In this chapter, we will cover:

- ▸ Selecting recent comments for a specific node type
- ▸ Focusing on the Archive view
- ▸ Filtering the backlinks
- ▸ Changing the Frontpage view
- ▸ Selecting the Glossary view entries for a specific user
- ▸ Creating an Attached Menu for the Taxonomy Term view
- ▸ Reporting Tracker activity for a certain user role

Introduction

The **Views** module comes with a number of useful predefined views. You can not only use them, but also edit them to meet whatever special needs arise.

Since these views are ready to use the moment the module is enabled, the steps necessary to make some changes to them are less than those needed to create new custom views, so these views are a logical choice for our first chapter.

Selecting recent comments for a specific node type

The **Recent Comments** view provides a block containing comments, which links to a page providing additional comment content. We will edit this view to enable us to display comments for a specific content type.

Getting ready

1. Ensure that your site has at least two types of content (the default **Page** and **Article** types are fine) and that you have access to each of these content types. Also, ensure that the content you wish to use has comments.

2. Navigate to the **Views** page (`admin/structure/views`) and click on the **Enable** link for the recent comments view.

3. Click on the **Clone** link that now appears for the view.

4. Enter **Article Comments Recent** as the view name.

5. Enter **Display comments for recent articles** as the view description.

6. Click on the **Next** button.

7. Click on the **Save** button at the bottom of the page.

How to do it...

We will edit the clone that we have created, and make some modifications to it to provide a new view. Carry out the following steps in order to accomplish this recipe:

1. Edit the recent view for article comments that we have created.

2. Click on the **+** link in the **Filters** box.

3. A dialog box titled **Master: Add filters** will open.

4. In the **Groups** select box, choose **Node**.

5. Scroll down to the **Node: Type** checkbox and check it; click on the **Add** button at the bottom of the **Add filters** dialog box to reveal the configuration box for the filter.

6. Click on the checkbox next to the content type you want to select. In our case, we will click on the one next to **Article**.

7. Make sure that **Node** is shown in the **Relationship** select box. Now, click on the **Update** button.

8. Click on the **Title** link in the **Title** box and change the title to **Recent article comments**, and then click on the **Update** button.

9. At the top of the page, select the **Page display** option.

10. Click on **Path** in the **Page settings** block, change the path to `article-comments-recent`, and click on the **Update** button.

11. At the top of the page, select the **Block display** option.

12. Click **Admin** in the **Block settings** block, change the **Block admin** description to **Recent article comments view**, and click on the **Update** button.

13. Click on the **Save** button.

14. The output of our view can be viewed at **article-comments-recent**.

The following screenshot shows the **Recent article comments** view:

> ## Recent article comments
>
> * Reply to: Test article 1 *26 min 39 sec* ago
>   Love it

How it works...

Most of the views that you will create will probably be **Node** views—views that use nodes as the primary source of data. This view uses a different entity type: **comments**. The relationship that was already in place, links each selected comment to the node for which the comment was made.

The original filter limits the selection of comments to those nodes that are published, unless the user has admin capability, in which case all comments will be selected. We added another filter, which further limits the selection of comments made on articles; therefore, even though there was a piece of page content with a comment, it was not displayed. However, if we run the original view (`comment/recent`), we see the result as not having added the additional filter:

> ## Recent comments
>
> * Reply to: Test page 1 *33 min 31 sec* ago
>   Love this too
> * Reply to: Test article 1 *35 min 15 sec* ago
>   Love it

There's more...

As you have seen, more than one filter can be applied to the selection of content. One additional filter to consider is **Comment: In moderation**, which would limit the displayed comments to those that have been approved or not, depending on the chosen setting.

Focusing on the Archive view

The **Monthly archive** view displays a list of links that are the months in which the content was published. The following screenshot shows the monthly archive view:

Monthly archive
- July 2010 (3)
- June 2010 (1)

Each link leads to a page that presents teasers of each of the pieces of content published that month. We're going to add a filter to the view so that only the user's content is considered instead of the content of all users.

Getting ready

Carry out the following steps in order to get started:

1. Ensure that your site has content posted by more than one author (for testing purposes).
2. Navigate to the **Views** page (`admin/structure/views`) and click on the **Enable** link for the **Monthly archive** view.
3. Click on the **Clone** link that now appears on the view, enter **User archive** as the view name, enter **Display a list of months that link to content for that month** for the current user as the view description, and click on the **Next** button.

How to do it...

We will edit the clone that we have created, and make some modifications to it to provide a new view. Carry out the following steps in order to accomplish this recipe:

1. Click on the **+ Add** link in the **Filters** box, and a dialog box titled **Master: Add filters** will open.
2. Scroll down to **User: Current** and click on the checkbox, then click on the **Add** button.
3. Click on the **Is the logged in user** checkbox for a "yes", and then click on the **Update** button.

4. Click on the **Title** link in the **Basic settings** box, change the title to **User archive**, and click on the **Update** button.

5. Select the **Page display** option.

6. Click on **Path** in the **Page settings** block, change the path to **user-archive**, and click on the **Update** button.

7. Select the **Block display** option.

8. Click on the **Admin** in the **Block settings** block, change the **Block admin** description to **User archive list**, and click on the **Update** button.

9. Click on the **Save** button.

10. The output of our view can be viewed at the `user-archive` link.

How it works...

This is an example of a Node view—a view that uses nodes as the source of the data. The original filter limits the selection of comments to those nodes that are published, and produces a links list of the months for which there was content published. We add another filter, which further limits the selection to nodes created by the current user.

Filtering the backlinks

A **backlink** is a link on another page that points to the current page. When Drupal 7 indexes content for searching, the links in the content that lead to other pages on the same site are noted and stored in a database table for reference as backlinks.

The **Backlinks** view displays a list of nodes that contain links to the requested node. If no node has been requested, all backlinks are listed. We're going to create another version of this view, which will provide a teaser of the node along with links to the nodes that link to it.

Getting ready

Carry out the following steps in order to get started:

1. For testing purposes, ensure that there is at least one backlink in your content.

2. From the **Content** list, select the node for which there will be a backlink. Take note of its node ID by placing the mouse cursor over its name and looking at the link information displayed, as shown in the following screenshot:

	TITLE	TYPE	AUTHOR	STATUS	UPDATED ▼	OPERATIONS
☐	DH777777 new	Home	ayen	published	03/05/2011 – 16:39	edit delete
☐	WH888888 new	Home	ayen	published	03/05/2011 – 16:38	edit delete
☐	M999999 new	Home	ayen	published	03/05/2011 – 16:37	edit delete
☐	Kidney chest new	Product	ayen	published	03/05/2011 – 01:02	edit delete
☐	Hand-carved Floor Mirror new		ayen	published	03/05/2011 – 01:02	edit delete
☐	Packt Publishing new	Spo	ayen	published	02/23/2011 –	edit

http://localhost/drupal/d7/node/80

3. Select a piece of content in which you will add a link. In the body of that content, add the link. In the preceding example, a link to **Test Page 1** would be as follows:

```
<a href="node/4">link to Test Page 1</a>
```

4. Run the `cron` command from the admin status report. Check the admin search settings to ensure that 100% of your content has been indexed. If not, run the `cron` command again. The following screenshot shows the indexing status:

> **INDEXING STATUS**
>
> *100%* of the site has been indexed. There are 0 items left to index.

5. Navigate to the **Views** page (`admin/structure/views`) and click on the **Enable** link for the Backlinks view. Click on the **Clone** link that now appears for the view.

6. Enter **teasers_with_backlinks** for the view name.

7. Enter **Displays a list of nodes that link to the node, using the search backlinks table** as the view description.

8. Click on the **Next** button.

9. Click on the **Save** button at the bottom of the page.

How to do it...

We will edit the clone we have created, and make some modifications to it to provide a new view. Carry out the following steps in order to accomplish this recipe:

1. Edit the teasers_with_backlinks view that we have created.

2. Click on the **HTML List** link next to **Format:** in the **Format settings** box.

3. Scroll down to the **Master: How should this view be styled** configuration box and select **Unformatted**, and then click on the **Update** button.

4. A subsequent configuration box, **Master: Style options,** opens. Click on the **Update** button.

5. Select the **Page display**.

6. Click on the **+** icon in the **Fields** box.

7. Scroll down to the configuration box, select **Fields** from the selected box. Select **Fields: body**, and click on the **Add** button.

8. In the subsequent configuration box, and clear the **Label** textbox, ensure that the **Formatter** select box contains **Summary or trimmed**, and click on the **Update** button.

9. Click on the **node/%/backlinks** link for Path in the **Page settings** box, change the URL to node/%/teasers-with-backlinks, and click on the **Update** button.

10. Click on the **Tab: What links ...** link for **Menu** in the **Page settings** box. Change the **Title** textbox contents to **A peek at what links here**. Enter **99** in the **Weight** textbox and click on the **Update** button.

11. Select **Block display** and click on the **What links here** link in the **Block settings** box. Change the contents of the textbox to **Teasers of what links here** and click on the **Update** button.

12. Click on the **Save** button.

13. We can view the altered node page by viewing the node that we know has other content linking to it; the example here is node/4:

14. Click on the link **A peek at what links here** (shown in the preceding screenshot) and you will be shown a teaser for each of the pieces of content that link to the one you were viewing, as shown in the following screenshot:

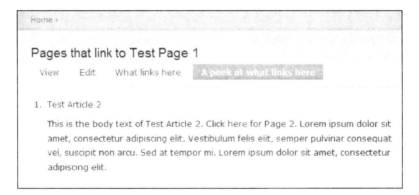

How it works...

This is an example of a Node view. The original view adds a tab to the node view, **What links here**, which gives a list of other nodes that link to the node being viewed. We added the node body as another field, which additionally displays a teaser for each of the nodes containing backlinks.

Changing the Frontpage view

The composition of the front (home) page in Drupal can be themed to alter its appearance, but the structure and sources of its content are pretty much determined for you. If you leave things as they are, the content area of the front page will consist of whatever nodes you have promoted, in any quantity up to the maximum that you set, and that's pretty much the extent of your control.

We're going to create a new front page that resembles the default **Frontpage** view only that it does display some content.

Getting ready

Carry out the following steps in order to get started:

For this recipe, we're going to be using a custom content type: **Gallery**, the details of which are given in *Appendix B, Entity Types and Fields*. Feel free to duplicate it, or create a content type more meaningful to you, or just use one of the existing content types. The content type also makes use of an image style so that the image in each piece of content can be presented in a uniform manner.

1. Create two entries of the content type that you choose to use.

2. Navigate to the **Views** page (`admin/structure/views`) and click on the **Enable** link for the frontpage view.

3. Click on the **Clone** link that now appears for the view.

4. Enter **alternate_frontpage** for the view name, **A different front page** as the view description, and click on the **Next** button.

5. Click on the **Save** button at the bottom of the page.

How to do it...

We will edit the clone we have created, and make some modifications to it to provide a new view. Carry out the following steps in order to accomplish this recipe:

1. Edit the alternate_frontpage view that we have created.

2. Click on **Paged, 10 items next to User** pager in the **Basic settings** box, select **Page output, Mini** pager, and click on the **Update** button.

3. Change **Items per page** to **1** and click on the **Update** button.

4. Click on the **+** icon in the **Filters** box.

5. Scroll down to the configuration box and select **Node** from the **Group** select box, scroll down and check the **Node: Type** checkbox, and click on the **Add** button.

6. A new configuration box opens. Check the **Gallery** checkbox below **Node type** and click on the **Update** button.

7. Click on the **Save** button.

8. Navigate to the admin **Configuration** page (admin/config) and click on **Site information**.

9. In the textbox for **Default front page**, change **node** to **frontpage** and click on the **Save configuration** button.

10. Navigate to the site root to view the page, which is shown in the following screenshot:

Mona Lisa

published by ay en on Thu, 02/03/2011 - 01:33

Sixteenth-century portrait painted in Florence, Italy by Leonardo di ser Piero da Vinci

11. Clicking the pager will load the next piece of content:

Heracles

published by j ayen green on Thu, 02/03/2011 - 01:33

by Philippe-Laurent Roland, 1806
Photo © Marie-Lan Nguyen / Wikimedia Commons

How it works...

The default version of the frontpage view is designed to provide precisely what the Drupal front page does. We created a view that shows content only of the custom Gallery type, composed primarily of an image, with one piece of content per page. Then we let Drupal know that this new view should be used as our front page.

Selecting the Glossary view entries for a specific user

The **Glossary** view presents a list of all content organized by the first letter of the title. This is a convenient view for site visitors that know the name of the content they are seeking, or who simply want to browse. We're going to give the user the ability to browse the content created by a specific author.

Getting ready

Carry out the following steps in order to get started:

1. Ensure that your site has content posted by more than one author (for testing purposes).
2. Navigate to the **Views** page (`admin/structure/views`) and click on the **Enable** link for the **Glossary** view.
3. Click on the **Clone** link that now appears for the view.
4. Enter **author_glossary** for the view name.
5. Enter **A list of all content, by letter, with author selection** as the view description.
6. Click on the **Next** button.
7. Click on the **Save** button at the bottom of the page.

How to do it...

The Glossary view, and now the clone that we created, has three displays: the **default** display, the **page** display that lists content, and an **attachment** display that lists each letter of the alphabet for which there is content along with the number of nodes. We will make some changes to the existing displays and create an additional one that will provide the author list.

Carry out the following steps in order to accomplish this recipe:

1. Edit the author_glossary view that we have created.
2. Click on the **+Add** link at the top of the page and select **Attachment** from the list. Then select the new **Attachment 2**.
3. Click on the **+** icon in the **Sort criteria** box, check the **User: Name** checkbox, and click on the **Add** button. A new configuration box will open. Select **Sort ascending**, click on the **Override** button and click on the **Update** button.
4. In the **Attachment settings** dialog box, click on **Before next to Position:**, select **After** in the configuration box, and click on the **Update** button.

5. Click **None** next to **Attach to:** in the **Attachment settings** dialog box, check the **Page** checkbox, and click on the **Update** button.

6. In the **Fields** box select each field one at a time other than **User: Name**, and in their settings box click on the **Remove** button, taking care to first select **Override** in the settings of the first field that you select.

7. Click **None** next to **Attach to:** in the **Attachment settings** dialog box, check the **Page** checkbox in the configuration box, and click on the **Update** button.

8. Click on the link next to **Query settings** in the **Other** box, check the **Distinct** check checkbox in the configuration box, and click on the **Update** button.

That is the work needed for the attachment itself. Now, we need to make a few minor changes to the settings from the original view.

1. Select the **Master** display.

2. Click on the **+** icon in the **Dynamic filters** box, select **User** from the select box in the configuration box, check the box next to **User: Name,** and click on the **Add** button.

3. In the subsequent configuration box,in the **Title** box, enter **Content starting with %1 for %2** and click on the **Update default display** button.

4. Select the **Page** display.

5. Click on the **glossary** link next to **Path:** in the **Page settings** box, change the path to **author-glossary**.

6. Click on the link next to **Menu** in the same box and change the title from **Glossary** to **Author Glossary**.

7. Click on the **Save** button.

8. Navigate to the home page, and first invoke the view simply by clicking on the **Author Glossary** link in the navigation menu. Notice the new attachment below the list of content. Your screen will vary from the following screenshot, based on the authors listed in your site:

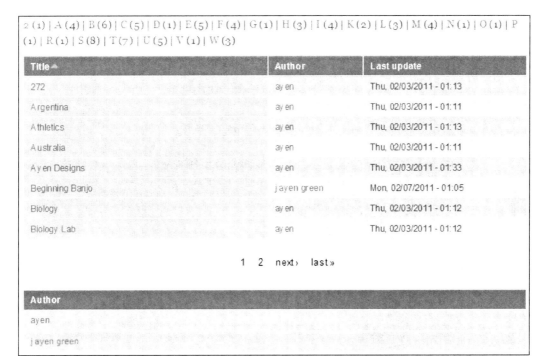

2 (1) | A (4) | B (6) | C (5) | D (1) | E (5) | F (4) | G (1) | H (3) | I (4) | K (2) | L (3) | M (4) | N (1) | O (1) | P (1) | R (1) | S (8) | T (7) | U (5) | V (1) | W (3)

Title ▲	Author	Last update
272	ay en	Thu, 02/03/2011 - 01:13
Argentina	ay en	Thu, 02/03/2011 - 01:11
Athletics	ay en	Thu, 02/03/2011 - 01:13
Australia	ay en	Thu, 02/03/2011 - 01:11
Ay en Designs	ay en	Thu, 02/03/2011 - 01:33
Beginning Banjo	j ayen green	Mon, 02/07/2011 - 01:05
Biology	ay en	Thu, 02/03/2011 - 01:12
Biology Lab	ay en	Thu, 02/03/2011 - 01:12

1 2 next › last »

Author
ay en
j ayen green

9. Then, click on the name of an author in the author attachment.

Content for j ayen green

Author	Title ▲	Last update
j ayen green	Beginning Banjo	Mon, 02/07/2011 - 01:05
j ayen green	Heracles	Mon, 02/07/2011 - 01:27

10. And finally, add **/x** to the end of the URL, where **x** is the first letter or word of a piece of that author's content that is not his first piece, alphabetically, which in my case will be **author-glossary/b/j ayen green**, as shown in the following screenshot:

Content for j ayen green starting with B

Author	Title ▲	Last update
j ayen green	Beginning Banjo	Mon, 02/07/2011 - 01:05

How it works...

We added a new attachment display to the existing view, giving it three displays. The first is the page display, which is the section of the view containing the information about content. The second is the original attachment, which appears first on the page, and is formatted as a summary of the available titles using the first letter of the title, and giving a total for each letter. The new attachment appears last, and contains the names of each author with authored content on the site.

We specified that the new attachment would inherit two arguments from the page display (which receives the arguments), those being the additional portions of the URL. The first argument is the title of a piece of content, or 'all' to specify that all should be used. The second argument is the name of an author, or is omitted entirely for all authors to be selected.

The link produced for each author name links back to the same view, providing 'all' as the title being searched (so, all titles) and the author's name. Thus, the page URL when selected from the menu item appears as author_glossary with no arguments, in which case all records are retrieved, and when an author link is clicked, `author_glossary/all/ author_name`, where all titles belonging to that author are retrieved. Finally, we entered `author_glossary/b/j ayen green` so that all titles beginning with B and authored by J. Ayen Green were retrieved.

There's more...

Attachment displays are a boon to the value of your views and your site. You can find several examples of their power in my book on *"Drupal 6 Attachment Views"*, *Packt Publishing*.

Creating an Attached Menu for the Taxonomy Term view

It's nice to be able to add meaningful content to a view, such as content used as a menu; but how do we do that without it being repeated with every record and still containing its own view content? An **Attachment** view can be used for this.

Getting ready

Carry out the following steps in order to get started:

1. Ensure that some of your content has taxonomy terms assigned to it.
2. Navigate to the **Views** page (`admin/structure/views`) and click on the **Enable** link for the taxonomy_term view.
3. Click on the **Clone** link that now appears for the view.

4. Enter **taxonomy_term_menu** for the view name.

5. Enter **Access content via a taxonomy term menu** as the view description.

6. Click on the **Next** button.

7. The view has two additional feeds that we do not need, so let's remove them. Click on the tab for the **Feed 1 display** and then the **Delete** button. Do the same for **Feed 2 display**.

 The displays may remain visible until the view is saved in the next step.

8. Click on the **Save** button at the bottom of the page.

How to do it...

We will be adding an attachment display that will be used as a menu to the existing view. Carry out the following steps in order to accomplish this recipe:

1. Edit the taxonomy_term_menu view that we have created.

2. Click on the **+ Add** button in the display list and add an **Attachment** display.

3. Click on the **Content** next to **Show:** in the **Format** checkbox, change the setting to **Fields**, click on the **Update and Override** button, and then the **Update** button in the subsequent configuration box.

4. Click on the **+** icon in the **Fields** box, scroll down to **Taxonomy: All terms** and check the box, then click on the **Add** button.

5. In the subsequent settings box, clear the **Label** text field.

6. Check the **Output this field as a link** checkbox in the **Rewriting** section of the same settings box, and enter **taxonomy/term-menu/[tid-term]** as the link path.

7. Check the **Hide if empty** checkbox in the **Empty Field Behavior** settings section.

8. In the **Display type** section, select **Simple separator**, enter **|** with a blank space before and after it into the **Separator** textbox, clear the **Link this field to its term page** checkbox, and click on the **Update and Override** button.

9. Click on the links for each of the two dynamic filters; click on the **Override** button (will appear for just the first filter chosen) and then on the **Remove** button to remove both.

10. In the same way, click on the links for each of the **Sort** criteria. Click **Override for the first**, and remove both. Then click on the icon to add a sort criterion and select the **Taxonomy: Term** field. Click on the **Update and Override** button.

11. Ensure **Ascending** is selected in the subsequent settings box, and then click on the **Update** button.

Those changes took care of the data requirements for the new Attachment display. Now, we need to make some changes to the structural parts of it before we finish.

1. Click on the settings gear icon next to **Paged, 10** items in the **Basic** settings box, change the **10** to **0**, and click on the **Update and Override** button.

2. Click on the **Title** link in the **Title** box and for the title, enter **Terms**. Then click on the **Update and Override** button.

3. Click on the **Content** next to **Show:** in the **Format** box, change the setting to **Fields**, click on the **Update and Override** button, and then the **Update** button in the subsequent configuration box.

4. In the **Attachment settings** box, click on the **Yes** link next to **Inherit arguments** and change the setting to **No**, then click on the **Update** button.

5. Click on the **None** link next to **Attach to** in the **Attachment** settings box. Check the box for **Page** and then click on the **Update** button.

6. Almost done now. The original view had dynamic filters that we have removed. We need to add a new one now.

7. Click on the **Page 1** button to change to the **Page** display.

8. Click on the **+** link for Dynamic filters, check the box for **Taxonomy: Term**, then click on the **Update and Override** button.

9. Click on the **Save** button and navigate to `taxonomy/term-menu` to see the results, as shown in the following screenshot:

black | blue | green | red | yellow

Water Lilies

published by ayen on Thu 02/03/2011 - 01:33

Oil on canvas by French Impressionist Claude Monet.

Chagall's Windows

published by ayen on Thu, 02/03/2011 - 01:33

Stained glass windows by Marc Chagall.

How it works...

Content can have taxonomy terms, often known as "tags" associated with it. We took a view that uses a node's taxonomy in a different way and edited it to present the terms associated with published nodes as a menu from which we can choose one as a filter. Most of the work we did was removing settings we would not need or adding new ones. The three primary changes were adding the attachment display to use as a menu, changing the dynamic filter for the page display to be the taxonomy term that we selected via its link, and setting the term to output in the attachment display as a link pointing back to our view along with the term name appended.

Drupal treats additional information in a URL as arguments, so, for example, if a page address is `my/page` and the URL is `my/page/2/even`, then the values `2` and `even` are processed as arguments, or parameters, to be passed to the page.

There's more...

The next few steps for a real site would be to theme the attachment display, perhaps add a pager for both, and maybe to change the position setting for the attachment display to 'after' rather than 'before', or even to have it appear side by side with the content.

Reporting Tracker activity for a certain user role

The default **Tracker** view lists the posts created by users. We will create an exposed filter to allow the admin to filter the view by user role. Filters require certain criteria to be met in order for records to be selected. Often, the value of the filter is one that can remain constant, such as requiring that content be published in order to be visible. There are times, however, when you will want the ability to change the value that is filtered. Rather than having to edit the view each time you want this value to change, you can simply elect to have the view provide a widget with which the value can be supplied.

Getting ready

Carry out the following steps in order to get started:

1. Ensure that your site has content posted by more than one author, and that the authors represent more than one role.
2. Navigate to the **Views** page (`admin/structure/views`) and click on the **Enable** link for the Tracker view.

3. Click on the **Clone** link that now appears on the view.

4. Enter **tracker_role** as the view name.

5. Enter **Shows all new activity on system by role** as the view description.

6. Click on the **Next** button.

7. Click on the **Save** button at the bottom of the page.

How to do it...

Carry out the following steps in order to accomplish this recipe:

1. Edit the tracker_role view that we have created.

2. Click on the **+** icon in the Filters box.

3. Check the **User: Roles** checkbox and click on the **Add** button.

4. A new configuration box will open. Click on the **Expose** button, uncheck the **Force single** checkbox if it is checked, then click on the **Update** button.

5. Select the **Page** display.

6. Click the tracker next to **Path:** in the **Page settings** box, change the path to **tracker_role** and click on the **Update** button.

7. Click **Normal: Recent** next to **Menu:** in the **Page settings** box. Change the **Title** to **Recent posts with selectable role** and click on the **Update** button.

8. Click on the link for the current Dynamic filters and then the **Remove** button.

9. Click on the **+** link in the **Dynamic filters** box, check the box for **User: roles**, click on the **Update default display**, and then the **Update** button in the subsequent configuration box.

10. Click on the **Save** button.

11. Navigate to **tracker_role** and you will see the exposed filter, as shown in the following screenshot, which you can use to choose to see nodes created by users of a specific role:

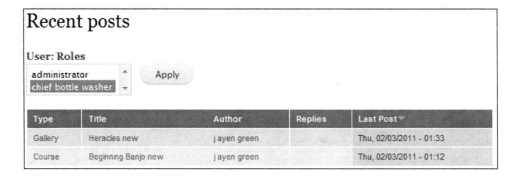

How it works...

We changed the Dynamic filter for the view to use the author's role rather than the original setting. We also created an attachment display and configured it to provide a list of user roles. Because this is a node view and not a user view, the information will be coming from content records and not user records, which means that the list will only contain roles for which content exists. In choosing the role in the exposed filter, its `rid` (role ID) that gets passed in the URL back to the view, which will then list only the content that has been created by a user with that role.

2
Basic Custom Views

In this chapter, we will cover:

- ▸ Selecting all the nodes
- ▸ Creating a Paged block display
- ▸ Creating a Dynamic Links display block
- ▸ Creating a Random Ad block
- ▸ Using a View Content filter
- ▸ Providing a user view for administrators
- ▸ Winning that argument
- ▸ Using Views to create a bulleted list
- ▸ Creating bulleted lists using multiple content types

Introduction

In this chapter we are going to begin creating custom views. We will be working with simple examples, which you can then alter, expand on, or combine to suit your own needs.

Selecting all the nodes

Normally, you will want to select only published nodes, because you only want users to see nodes that have been published. However, as an admin, you could very well want to view unpublished nodes as well. Fortunately, there is a way to account for both requirements using a filter made just for this job.

Getting ready

Ensure that your site has both published and unpublished content.

How to do it...

Carry out the following steps on the **Views List** page in order to accomplish this recipe:

1. Navigate to the **Views List** page (`admin/structure/views`).
2. Click on the **+Add new view** link. Enter **Browse all nodes** as the **View name**. Check the **Description** box and enter **Browse all content if admin, all published if not**.
3. Enter **Browse content** as the Page title. In the Display format select boxes, select **Unformatted list, teasers, without links,** and **without comments**, respectively.
4. Check the **Create a menu link** checkbox, select the **Main** menu, enter **Browse content** as the menu text, and then click on the **Continue and edit** button.

Carry out the following steps on the **Views Edit** page:

1. Click on the **Add** link in the **Filter Criteria** panel, check the box next to **Content Published or Admin**, click on the **Add and configure filter criteria** button, and click on the **Apply** button in the subsequent configuration box.
2. Click on the **Save** button at the top of the screen.
3. Navigate to the front page.
4. Click on the **Browse content** menu tab while logged in as the admin—the unpublished nodes will typically show as pink unless this has been overridden in your theme. This is shown in the following screenshot:

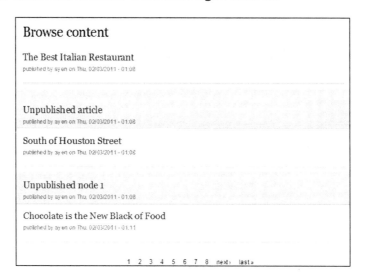

5. Now, log out and click on the **Browse content** link again. You are now seeing this view as a site visitor would, and only the published nodes are shown:

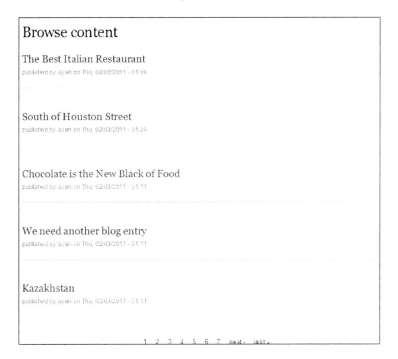

How it works...

By default, a node view will select all available nodes, with no filtering at all. It will sort them starting from the most recent one. Also, a node view will default to show selected fields rather than the entire node. We changed our view to select all nodes if the user, who is selecting the view, is the admin, but only published nodes in other cases. We then changed the style of the output to present the nodes as teasers instead of fields, and finally, we created a page display, assigned a path to it (/browse), and added it to the site's main menu.

There's more...

The main concept to take away from this view is the use of a filter. There are many criteria on which a view can be filtered, and we will use several criteria throughout the book. Also, more than one filter can be applied to the same display. For example, in addition to the filter we added, we could have also required the node to have been promoted to the front page, and even selected a specific node type.

Creating a Paged block display

The output presented by a view is typically seen in the content area of the page, but views are also capable of creating displays that appear as blocks in any selectable region of your theme. We are going to create a block that provides a paged display of content for a specific content type.

Block displays

The next few recipes make use of block displays. The block displays of views are not necessarily any different than manually constructed blocks in appearance. The difference is that their content is dynamic. Technically, the block does not exist until the page is created (an exception being that if caching is used, the block does exist in cache). At that point, the data for it is retrieved from the database, and the block is then rendered.

Getting ready

This recipe uses a custom content type, **Sponsor**, the details of which are in *Appendix B, Entity Types and Fields*. We will create a few nodes of this content type.

How to do it...

Carry out the following steps on the **Views List** page in order to accomplish this recipe:

1. Navigate to the **Views List** (admin/structure/views). Click on the **+Add new view** link. Enter **Sponsors** as the **View name**. Check the **Description** box and enter **Views related to Event sponsors**. Check the box for **Create a block**, enter **Our Sponsor...** as the **Block title**.

2. In the **Display format** select boxes, select **unformatted list, teasers, without links,** and **without comments**, respectively. Now, click on the **Continue and edit** button.

That creates the view, and now we need the view to do something, so on the **View Edit** page: carry out the following steps

1. Click on the **Add** link in the **Filter Criteria** panel; check the box next to **Content Type** and the one next to **Content Published or Admin**. Click on the **Add and configure filter criteria** button, check the box for **Sponsor**, click on the **Apply** button, and click it again for the **Content Published or Admin** configuration box.

2. Click **Paged, 10 items** next to **Use pager:** in the **Pager** box. Select **Paged output, mini pager** in the **configuration** box, set the pager number to **1**, and click on the **Update and continue** button.

3. Click on the **Save** button.

4. Navigate to the **Blocks Admin** page (`admin/structure/block`).

5. Scroll down to **Sponsor ad** in the **Disabled** section.

6. Select the **Right** sidebar from the select box.

7. Click on the **Save blocks** button.

8. Navigate to the front page to view the block, which should look similar to the following screenshot:

How it works...

We have created a node view, and limited its selection to the Sponsor content type nodes that are published (or all nodes, in the case of the user being an admin). We set the maximum record to 1, which will first show the most recent node of that type.

 We changed the pager number to 1, because it is likely that the content area will be using pager 0, and each pager on a page must have a unique number.

We changed the row type to node, so that we will receive a teaser display of the one node shown. We specified that one record be shown at a time, with a mini pager below it for navigation. We assigned the block to the right sidebar. If there are 10 nodes that meet our criteria, each will be shown in turn as the pager is clicked.

Using Override

When making a settings change on a display other than the Master display, decide whether the change should affect all displays or only the display being edited. If you want to make changes only to the display being edited, be sure to click on the **Override** button if it is present before adding or updating the display.

Creating a Dynamic Links display block

Views are capable of creating displays that appear as blocks in any selectable region of your theme. We are going to create a block that provides a dynamic list of links for a specific content type.

Getting ready

This recipe uses a custom content type, **Sponsor**, the details of which are present in *Appendix B, Entity Types and Fields*. We will create a few nodes of this content type.

How to do it...

[This recipe is based on the view created in the previous recipe.]

Carry out the following steps on the **Views List** page in order to accomplish this recipe:

1. Navigate to the **Views List** (admin/structure/views).
2. Click on the **Edit** link for the **Sponsors** view.

Carry out the following steps on the **View Edit** page:

1. Click on the **+ Add** link next to the **Block display** button at the top of the page.
2. Click on the link besides **Admin** and enter **Sponsor Links Block** as the block name in the text box that appears.
3. Click on the **Add link** in the **Filter Criteria** panel, check the box next to **Content Type** and the one next to **Content Published or Admin**. Click on the **Add and configure filter criteria** button, check the box for **Sponsor**, and click on the **Apply** button. Click it again for the **Content Published or Admin configuration** box.
4. Click **Paged, 10 items** next to **Use pager:** in the **Pager** box, select **Specified number of items** in the configuration box, change the number of items to **5**, set the offset to **1**, and click on the **Update and continue** button.
5. Click on the **Save** button and navigate to the **Blocks Admin** page (admin/ structure/block).
6. Scroll down to the **Sponsor links** block in the **Disabled** section. Select the **Right sidebar** from the select box and click on the **Save blocks** button.

7. Navigate to the front page to view the block, as shown in the following screenshot:

> Sponsor links block
>
> Packt Publishing
>
> A publisher of Drupal and
> other technical books.
>
>
> TheAccidentalCoder.com
>
> A Drupal and
> programming blog from
> which the occasional
> valuable nugget can be
> gleaned.

How it works...

We used the node view that we had created in the preceding recipe. We also created an additional block display and limited its selection to the Sponsor content type nodes that are already published (or all the nodes if the user is admin). We set the maximum records to be shown as 5, which will be the most recent nodes of that type. We then set the offset to 1. The reason for this is that the **Sponsor ad** block from the preceding recipe will display the most recent sponsor node, so it does not need to be included; the offset setting will have views skip one record and start the list with the second most recent sponsor.

Creating a Random Ad block

Anyone who has spent time on the web has seen advertisements, usually in the form of banners. In a Drupal site, an ad is typically in a block, which is mostly a region of the screen other than the main content area. Adding content to a block manually results in a static ad, which could be all that is required, but if dynamic ads are needed, creating a view with a block display is the way to go. We are going to create a block that presents an ad for a randomly-selected product and display it in the content area.

Getting ready

This recipe uses a custom content type, **Product**, the details of which are in *Appendix B, Entity Types and Fields*. Create at least one node of this content type, or more if you want to see the random selection at work.

How to do it...

Carry out the following steps in order to accomplish this recipe:

1. Navigate to the **Views List** page (`admin/structure/views`). Click on the **+Add new view** link, and enter **Product ads** as the **View name**.

2. Check the **Description** box and enter **Random product ad block**.

3. Select **Content** from the **Show** list and select the type to be **Product**.

4. Check the box for **Create a block**.

5. In the **Display format** select boxes, select **unformatted list, teasers, without links**, and **without comments** respectively. Set the **Items per page** to **1** and click on the **Continue and edit** button.

That creates the view, and now we just need to add a few settings:

1. Click on the **Add** link in the **Sort criteria** box and select **Global: Random**.

2. Click on the **Add and configure sort criteria** button.

3. Click on the **Apply** button and save the changes.

4. Navigate to the **Blocks Admin** page (`admin/structure/block`).

5. Scroll down to **Random ad** in the **Disabled** section, select **Content** from the select box, and click on the **Save blocks** button.

6. Navigate to the front page to view the block, as shown in the following screenshot:

How it works...

We created a node view, and limited its selection to Product content type nodes. We set the sort option to random, which means that Drupal will randomly select a record for use. We set the maximum records to 1, so that only one product is shown. We specified that the format should be a node teaser, so we see the title, description, price, and image. At that point, if we had created a page display then the view would have been displayed on that page. Instead, we created a block display and assigned the block to the content area so that it shows along with the main content.

There's more...

In *Chapter 5*, *Intermediate Custom Theming Views*, we will cover the *Theming a view page* recipe. The current format of this view cries out for theming, such as making the price larger and floating the text next to the image.

Using a View Content filter

Often, the quantity of content can be overwhelming to navigate, when browsing through it page by page. Filtering allows the content selection to be reduced using specific criteria. We will create a view that allows the user to filter the content.

Getting ready

This recipe uses a custom content type, Home, the details of which are in *Appendix B, Entity Types and Fields*. We will create at least two nodes of this content type, each with a different zip code.

How to do it...

Carry out the following steps in order to accomplish this recipe:

1. Navigate to the **Views List** (admin/structure/views).
2. Click on the **+Add** new view link.
3. Enter **Homes for sale** as the **View name**.
4. Check the **Description** box and enter **Homes for sale** as the description in the text box that appears.
5. Select **Content** from the **Show** list and select the type to be **Home**.
6. In the **Display format** select boxes, select **unformatted list, teasers, with links**, and **without comments** respectively, and then click on the **Continue and edit** button.

Having created the view, we need to add a few settings:

1. Click on the **Add** link next to **Fields**.
2. Check the box next to **Fields: field_zip_code**. Click on the **Add and configure fields** button.
3. In the configuration box for **field_zip_code**, click on the **Expose Filter** button. Ensure that the checkbox for **Required** is not checked, check the **Expose the operator** checkbox, change the **Label** to **Zip code**, and then click on the **OK** button.
4. Click **None** next to **Title**, enter **Homes for sale** in the textbox, and click on the **Update** button.
5. Click **None** next to **Path:** in the **Page settings** section, enter **homes** in the textbox, and click on the **Update** button.
6. Click on the **Save** button and navigate to **homes**.

7. We can select **Is not empty** from the **Zip code filter** select box and click on the **Apply** button, and receive all records. Alternatively, we can specify a zip code using another filter, such as **Is equal to** to limit the display, as shown in the following screenshot:

How it works...

A view is essentially one or several SQL statements, in terms of the data acquisition. In effect, a filter results in an equivalent WHERE clause being added to the SQL statement, to gather a subset of the available data. So, what we have done is created a view that gathers all the nodes. We reduced the number of nodes that the view will receive from the database by specifying that the nodes must be of the Home content type. Finally, we provided the means to select a focused subset of those records by allowing the user to specify a zip code and exposing the filter. By unlocking the operator in the filter, the user is free to request, for example, a specific zip code, zip codes greater than a value, all zip codes not equal to another value, or every zip code.

Providing a user view for administrators

Not every view needs to contain data visible to the general public. The user permissions functionality of views does not natively provide the granularity to allow only certain views to be seen. There is a way to do it, and it is quite simple. We will create a view that shows user data, and limits access to it to just the administrators.

How to do it...

Carry out the following steps on the **Views List** page in order to accomplish this recipe:

1. Navigate to the **Views List** (`admin/structure/views`), click on the **+Add new view** link, and enter **Users** as the **View name**.

2. Check the **Description** box and enter **User info** as the description in the text box that appears.

3. Select **Users** from the **Show** list and set **sorted by** to **Title**.

4. Enter **General user info** for the **Page** title, `admin/reports/general-user-info` as the path, and in the **Display format** select boxes, select **unformatted list, fields, without links**, and **without comments** respectively, and then click on the **Continue and edit** button.

We have created the view framework, and will now configure its settings to select the required information.

1. Check the box for the **Create a menu** link, select **Management** from the **Menu** select box, enter **General user info** in the **Menu label** textbox, and then click on the **Continue and edit** button.

2. Click on the **Add** link in the **Fields** box, check the boxes for **User: Active, User: Created date, User: E-mail, User: Edit link, User: Language, User: Last login, User: Name**, and **User: Roles**. Then click on the **Add and configure** button.

3. In the **User: Active** configuration box ensure **All displays** is selected at the top besides the **For link**, check the box for **Create a label,** and click on the **OK** button. Do the same for the **User: Created date** and **User: E-mail** fields, In the **User: Edit** link box, ensure **All displays** is selected at the top besides the **For link**, clear the **Create a label** textbox, enter **Edit user** in the **Text to display** textbox, and click on the **OK** button.

4. In the **User: Language** box ensure **All displays** is selected at the top, beside **For,** clear the Create a label textbox, enter **Edit user** in the Text to **display** textbox and click on the **OK** button. Do the same for **User: Name** and **User: Roles**.

5. In the **User: Last login** box ensure **All displays** is selected from the select box at the top beside the **For** link, and click on the **OK** button. Do the same for **User: Name** and **User: Roles**.

6. Click on the fields reorder icon (up and down arrows), drag **Name** to the top, **E-mail** under **Name**, **Created date** directly above **Last login**, **Edit link** to the bottom, and click on the **Apply** button.

7. Click on the **+** icon in the **Sort criteria** box, check the box next to **User: Name**, and click on the **Add** button.

8. Click on the **Not set next to Access:** link in the **Page settings** box, click on the **Role** radio button, click on the **Administrator** radio button, and click on the **Update** button.

9. Click on the **Analyze** button. The **Results** box should indicate that there is nothing to report. Now, click on the **OK** button.

10. Click on the **Save** button.

11. Navigate to the new report either by selecting it from the **Admin** menu, in which case it will display as an overlay, or by entering the URL (`admin/reports/general-user-info`). Try logging out and accessing it too. The report will look similar to the following screenshot:

How it works...

We started by creating a user view, rather than a content view as we have been doing. We did not set a filter, because in the case of a user view there are no content types to be concerned with and we wanted to retrieve all user records. We selected several fields from the user record and sorted them in a sensible order. We gave the view a path and assigned it to the **Management** menu. Finally, we specified that access to the view will be limited only to users with the administrator role. Three out of all the fields will be links without our having to do anything special to make them so; these are the **Edit** link, the **User name** link (a link to the user record), and the **E-mail address** link (a mailto: link).

There's more...

There is another method available for restricting access, and that is to select **Permission** instead of **Role** as the access setting. That choice provides a select box that lists the existing permissions from which the user can choose the permissions that are needed to access the view. However, there is no 'Add new permission' choice offered, and hence the usefulness depends on whether an existing permission already applies. Instead of selecting the administrator role, we could have selected the **Access all Views** permission. Usually, this is restricted to admins, but not necessarily, so the downside of using this would be that if the permissions were ever given to users other than administrators, then the view would no longer be restricted to administrators. On the other hand, having selected a role in the view means that administering the access to the view must be done in the view rather than through the permission system.

The output leaves much to be desired, aesthetically. In fact, with there being no spacing between user records, the very utility of the display is lessened. We will be learning about using a table format in the next chapter. Using that here would be an immediate improvement on the default output. In *Chapter 5, Intermediate Custom Theming Views*, we will cover the *Theming a view page* recipe, which is yet another way to improve the aesthetics. Here, our method will be making a couple of quick edits to give the view more utility.

The site theme already has a CSS file, and we could make the changes directly to it, but if we do that, the next time the theme has an update, our changes will be overwritten, so we will add a CSS file instead.

I am using the **Seven** theme that comes with Drupal 7. We will open the file seven.info in its directory (themes/seven). Make the following changes in the seven.info file.

Below the last line:

```
stylesheets[screen][] = style.css
```

Add the following lines of code:

```
stylesheets[screen][] = overrides.css
```

Now, open a new file and enter the following into it:

```
.page-admin-reports-general-user-info .views-row
{
  margin-bottom: 6px;
}
.page-admin-reports-general-user-info .views-row-odd
{
  background-color: #eee;
}
```

Save the file as `overrides.css` in the same theme folder. Clear the cache (`admin/config/development/performance`) and return to the report. Now the report is much easier to read, as shown in the following screenshot:

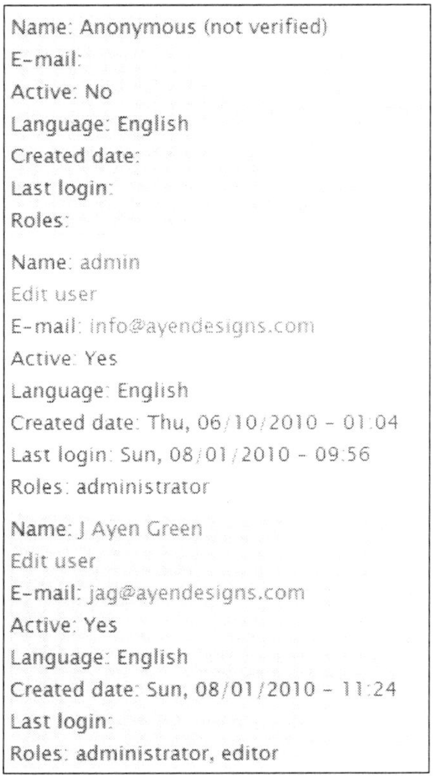

Name: Anonymous (not verified)
E-mail:
Active: No
Language: English
Created date:
Last login:
Roles:

Name: admin
Edit user
E-mail: info@ayendesigns.com
Active: Yes
Language: English
Created date: Thu, 06/10/2010 - 01:04
Last login: Sun, 08/01/2010 - 09:56
Roles: administrator

Name: J Ayen Green
Edit user
E-mail: jag@ayendesigns.com
Active: Yes
Language: English
Created date: Sun, 08/01/2010 - 11:24
Last login:
Roles: administrator, editor

Winning that argument

The node ID is a value that is unique to each piece of node content; in combination with a URL it provides a direct path to a node. But what if we want a query where the selection criteria changes rather than a link to a specific node? The answer to this is **dynamic fiters** (**arguments**). We will create a view that can interpret links containing a dynamic filter.

Getting ready

This recipe uses a custom content type, Home, the details of which are in *Appendix B, Entity Types and Fields*. We will create at least two nodes of this content type, each having a different zip code.

How to do it...

Carry out the following steps in order to accomplish this recipe:

1. Navigate to the **Views List** (`admin/structure/views`).
2. Click on the **+Add** new view link.
3. Enter **Homes links** as the **View name**.
4. Check the **Description** box and enter **Homes for sale** as the description in the text box that appears.
5. Select **Content** from the **Show** list and set **sorted by** to **Title**.
6. Enter **Homes for sale** for the **Page title**, **zip/%** as the **Path**, and in the **Display format** select boxes, select **unformatted list**, **teasers**, **without links**, and **without comments** respectively, and then click on the **Continue and edit** button.

We will now define the criteria for selecting records, in general.

1. Click on the **Add** link in the **Filter Criteria** panel, check the boxes next to **Node: Published** and **Node: Type**, then click on the **Add and configure filter criteria** button.
2. Click on the radio button for **Yes** in the configuration box that opens for **Node: Published** and click on the **Update** button.
3. Check the box for **Home** in the configuration box for **Node: Type** and click on the **Update** button.
4. Click on the **Add** link in the **Dynamic filters** box, check the box next to the **Fields: field_zip_code (field_zip_code) - value** (note that there are two fields with similar names), and click on the **Apply and continue** button.

5. In the resulting configuration box, in the section titled **WHEN THE FILTER IS IN THE URL OR A DEFAULT IS PROVIDED**, check the box for **Override title** and enter **Homes for sale in the %1 zip code**. Click on the **Apply** button, and then click on the **Save** button.

6. Navigate to `zip/{xxxxx}` (replace `{xxxxx}` with one of the zip codes in your sample data). A screen similar to the following screenshot will appear:

Homes for sale in the 20006 zip code

WH888888

132 rooms including 35 bathrooms, 55,000 square feet on 18 acres. Several previous residents. Guard booth and gate. Large kitchen.

Zip code: 20006

17 760 000.00

Read more

DH777777

237 rooms plus kitchens, maintenance, reception rooms and storage areas. All modern conveniences.

Zip code: 20006

37 000 000.00

Read more

How it works...

We created a basic content view, but instead of controlling the selection of data with an exposed filter, through which a user provides the filtering value, we used a dynamic filter, which allows the URL to provide the filter. The end result is the same in both cases, a URI value becoming a WHERE clause in the SQL that retrieves the data, but with this method the selection comes from links without user intervention.

There's more...

The decision to use a dynamic filter or an exposed filter, in this case, would be based on the intention. If it is to allow the user to select a zip code, we would instead have used an exposed filter. In our case, it is likely that there will be a list of locations serviced by the website, with each being a clickable link that provides the zip code to the view. Dynamic filters can accept more than one value, if configured. That way, if a location has more than one zip code, the URI could be something like `homes/12345+12346+12348`. This recipe was a simple example of using a single argument. The argument capabilities provided by views are quite sophisticated, with the ability to use multiple arguments, default arguments, various argument validation methods, and so on. Look for arguments to appear in subsequent recipes.

Using Views to create a bulleted list

There are a number of ways in which data can be presented with views. Sometimes the needs are quite simple, as is the case in this recipe. We will create a view that produces a block with a basic bulleted list.

The only requirement for this recipe is that there is published content available.

How to do it...

Carry out the following steps in order to accomplish this recipe:

1. Navigate to the **Views List** page (`admin/structure/views`).
2. Click on the **+Add** new view link.
3. Enter **Content topics** as the **View name**.
4. Check the **Description** box and enter **Bulleted list of topics**.
5. Select **Content** from the **Show** list and set **sorted by** to be **Title**.
6. Check the box for **Create a block**.
7. Enter **For your interest** as the **Block title**, and in the **Display format** select boxes, select **HTML list**, **titles**, **without links**, and **without comments** respectively, and then click on the **Continue and edit** button.

We have created the basic framework of our new view, and now need to establish the settings:

1. Click on the **Add** link in the **Filters** box, check the box next to **Node: Published**, and click on the **Apply and configure filters** button.
2. In the subsequent configuration box, click on the radio button for **Yes** and click on the **Apply** button.
3. Click on the **Add** link in the **Sort criteria** box, scroll down, and check the box next to **Global: Random**. Click on the **Configure sort criteria** button.

4. In the **Fields** box, click on the link for **Node: Title**, set the field to link to its content, clear the **Label** textbox, and click on the **Apply** button.

5. Click **None** next to **Admin:** in the **Block settings** box, enter **Contents bullet list** as the description, and click on the **Apply** button.

6. Click on the **Analyze** button. The results box should indicate that there is nothing to report. Click on the **OK** button and then click on the **Save** button.

7. Navigate to the **Blocks Admin** page (`admin/structure/block`), scroll down to the **Disabled** section, and set **Content bullets list** to **Sidebar** first. Now click on the **Save blocks** button.

8. Navigate to **Home** to view the block, as shown in the following screenshot:

How it works...

We create a very simple content view block display, which selects all published nodes of any type. We set the sort criteria to be random, so that any published node might appear on the first page of the block. We select one field to be shown, the node title, and set it to be displayed as a link to the node itself. The essential step for this recipe is setting the output format to that of an HTML unordered list.

There's more...

You might not want the block to contain items already present on the front page, particularly if the block only appears on the front page. In that case, an additional filter can be set for **Node: Promoted** and set to only select records that are not promoted to the front page.

Our list appears as a standard bulleted list because that is now the formatting for an unordered list defined in the active theme. By changing the definition of the `<ul>` (unordered list) and `<li>` (list item) tags in the theme `CSS` file, the bullets can be changed to another type, to images, removed altogether, or the items displayed inline rather than on separate lines.

Creating bulleted lists using multiple content types

There are a number of ways in which data can be presented with views. Sometimes the needs are quite simple, as is the case in this recipe. We will create a view that produces a block with a basic bulleted list. However, in this case we do not simply want one long list. We will create a list grouped under headings.

Getting ready

This recipe only requires that there is published content available of more than one content type.

How to do it...

Carry out the following steps in order to accomplish this recipe:

1. Navigate to the **Views List** page (`admin/structure/views`).
2. Click on the **+Add** new view link.
3. Enter **Grouped content topics** as the **View name**.
4. Check the **Description** box and enter **Bulleted list of topics**.
5. Select **Content** from the **Show** list.
6. Check the box for **Create a block**.
7. Enter **For your interest** as the **Block** title, and in the **Display format** select box, select **HTML list**, **titles**, **without links**, and **without comments** respectively, then click on the **Continue and edit** button.

We have created the basic framework of our new view, and now need to establish the settings:

1. Click on the **Add** link in the in the **Filters** box, check the box next to **Node: Published**, and click on the **Apply and configure filters** button.
2. In the subsequent configuration box, click on the radio button for **Yes** and the **Apply** button.
3. Click on the **Add** link in the in the **Fields** box and check the boxes for **Node: Type** and **Node: Title**, then click on the **Apply and configure fields** button.

4. In the configuration box for **Node: Title,** clear the **Label** box and make sure it is set to link to its content, then click **Apply**.

5. In the **Node: Type** configuration box check the box to **Exclude from display** and click on the **OK** button.

6. Click on the **Add** link in the in the **Sort criteria** box, scroll down and check the checkbox next to **Node: Type**, and click on the **Apply and configure sort criteria** button.

7. Do the same again but check the box for **Global: Random**.

8. Click on the **Unformatted** link in the **Style settings** box, change the formatting to **Table**, and click **Apply and continue**. Set **Group by** to **Type** and click **OK**.

9. Click **None** next to **Admin:** in the **Block settings** box, enter **Grouped contents bullet list** as the description, and click on the **Apply** button.

10. Click on **No** next to **Use grouping:** in the **Advanced settings** box. Check the **Group by** checkbox, and click on the **OK** button.

11. Click on the **Save** button.

12. Navigate to the **Blocks Admin** page (`admin/structure/block`), scroll down to the **Disabled** section and set **Grouped content bullets list** to **Sidebar** first, and then click on the **Save** blocks button.

13. Navigate to **Home** to view the block, as shown in the following screenshot:

How it works...

In this recipe, we essentially created the same view that we did previously, except for a few changes. We specified that the primary sort should be the content type. We also added **Node: Type** as a field. We set it to be excluded from display, so it would not be listed in the table as row data, but would still be available to be used as a heading. The most important change was specifying that the table can be grouped by the content type, which in turn segregated the output records.

3
Intermediate Custom Views

In this chapter, we will cover:

- Selecting node teasers based on types and contents
- Displaying a table of entity fields
- Sortable table with a header and footer
- Using AJAX for page changes
- Using relationships
- Grouping in a query
- Nodes within nodes
- Producing custom links
- Proving a negative with a filter and an argument

Introduction

In this chapter, we will continue creating custom views. We will learn how to make views more dynamic and rich. The views will also be more complex than those which we created in the previous chapter, making more use of the available Views' functionality.

Selecting node teasers based on types and contents

Sometimes, simply filtering by the content type is not sufficient. Filters can be combined to provide more than one selection criteria. We can select based on metadata, such as content type, and also on the content itself. In this recipe, we will select entries that are blog posts or other content having the same topic.

Getting ready

There are a few things we will need to prepare before beginning this view:

▸ If it is not already enabled, then enable the core Blog module at admin/modules

▸ Edit the Blog content type (created by the blog module)

▸ Click on the **Manage fields** tab

▸ In the **Add existing field** section, create a field Tags as a Term reference using an Autocomplete widget

▸ In the subsequent configuration dialog, simply click on the **Save** button

▸ Add a few blog posts using a small number of tags, and at least one other piece of non-blog content with that tag term in the content title

 For this example, we will be using the taxonomy term "food". Replace "food" in the instructions with whichever tag you used in creating your content.

How to do it...

On the **Views List** page:

1. Navigate to the **Views List** page (`admin/structure/views`) and click on the **+Add new view** link. Enter **Blog posts** as **View and name**, check the box for **Description**, enter **Subsets of blog posts** as **View description**, and click on the **Next** button.

2. The **Show** options should be **Content, Blog entry**, and **Newest first**. In the **Create a page** section, change the **Page title** to **Food blog posts** and the **Path of blog-posts** to **blog-posts/food**. In the **Display format** select boxes, change **with links** to **without** links. Click on the **Continue and edit button**.

3. At this point, we have defined the overall view, and now we can adjust its settings.

On the view's edit page:

1. Under the **Page** tab, click on the link next to **Display name**; at the top of the page, change **Page** to **Food** and click on the **Update** button.

2. Click on the **add** link besides **Filters Criteria**. Scroll down and check the box next to **NodeContent**: **Title**, and click on **Add and configure filter criteria**.

3. Click on the arrow next to the filters add link and select **and/or**.

   At this point, all three filters are being evaluated as And conditions, which means that all have to be true for a record to be selected. We want the filters for Content type and the Content title to be the OR condition, meaning if either of them is true, the record will be selected. In order to do this, we must reorganize the filters as follows.

4. Click on the **Add new filter group** link, drag the **Content**: **Type** and **Content**: **Title** filters down to the new group area, and then change the **And** setting to its left to **Or** and click on the **Apply** button.

5. In the **NodeConfigure filter criterion**: **Content**: Title configuration box, change the **Operator** select box to **Contains. Enter food** in the **Value textbox, and click on the Apply** button.

6. Click on **No menu** next to **Menu** in the **Page settings** box. Click on the radio button next to **Normal menu entry**. Enter **Food blog** in the **Title** textbox and click on the **Apply** button.

7   Click on the **Save** button.

8. Click on the **Analyze** button at the top of the page.

9. From the **Displays** list, click on the arrow next to **edit name and description**. The results box should indicate that there is nothing to report. Click on the **Ok** button.

10. Navigate to the menu editor (admin/structure/menu) and click on the **list links** link for the navigation menu.

11. Disable the **My blog** link (further down the list), drag **Food blog** to be under **Blogs**, and make sure that it has the same indentation as of the **My blog** entry. Enable **Blogs** (the **disabled** notation next to **Blogs** will not change until it is saved) and click on the **Save configuration** button. That portion of the menu list should now appear as shown in the following screenshot:

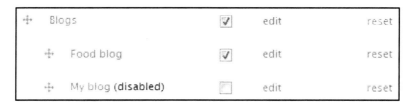

12. Navigate to the front page and click on the **Food blog** menu link, which will result in a blog entry, as shown in the following screenshot:

Food blog posts

Chocolate is the New Black of Food
published by ayen on Thu, 02/03/2011 - 01:11

Chocolate has a developed a bad reputation over the years...it's fattening, addicting, and high in calories. That said, recent evidence points to a small daily amount of dark chocolate having properties that contribute to good health.

We need another blog entry
published by ayen on Thu, 02/03/2011 - 01:11

Fresh Food - More Bang for the Buck!
published by ayen on Thu, 02/03/2011 - 01:08

Currently there is a renaissance of fresh food. Small local farms are popping up all over, giving more and more people the opportunity to purchase organic fruit and vegetables.

How it works...

By default, a content view will select all available node content with no filtering at all. It will sort, starting from the most recent.

We changed our view to filter based on the content type Blog, and also to filter on the content title containing the word 'food'. This filtering would normally result only in Blog content with the word 'food' in the title being selected. However, we gave the filters an OR relationship to each other, so the selection became Blog content OR content with 'food' in the title. This results in the article about fresh food being included because the word 'food' is present in its title, even though it is not a blog entry.

We assigned a path (`mydomain.com/blog/food`) to our page display and added it to the site's navigation menu.

There's more...

The main concept to take away from this view is the use of filters with an OR relationship. Any can be true, as opposed to in the AND relationship, where all the criteria needs to be true. We will see the OR filters again later in this book.

Displaying a table of entity fields

It is common for the output of a view to be in the form of a node or a node teaser, whether as part of a page or in a block. However, this is not the only format in which a view can present data. Sometimes, a user is able to absorb the data more easily with a more recognizable format, such as a table, and that is what we will create in this recipe.

Getting ready

- ▶ This recipe uses a custom content type, **Ingredient**, the details of which are in *Appendix B, Entity Types and Fields*
- ▶ Create a few nodes of this content type

How to do it...

On the **Views List** page:

1. Navigate to the Views **List page** (`admin/structure/views`) and click on the **+Add new view** link. Enter **shopping list** as the **View title**, **Shopping list** as the **View name**, check the box for **Description**, enter **A list of bulk ingredients** as the **View description**, and click on the **Next** button. The **Show** options should be **Content**, **Ingredient**, and **Title**.

2. In the **Display format**, select **Table** (the adjacent select boxes will disappear) and click on the **Continue and edit** button.

   At this point, we have defined the overall view, and now we can adjust its settings on the view edit page, as follows.

3. Click on the **add** link, next to **Fields**. Check the boxes for **Fields: Body**, **Fields: Measure**, and **Fields: Quantity**, and then click on the **Add and configure** button.

4. In the **Configure field Fields: Body** box, change the label from **Body** to **Notes**, then click on the **Apply and continue** button.

5. In the **Configure field Fields: Measure** box, change the label to **Unit of measure** and click on the **Apply and continue** button.

6. In the **Configure field Fields: Quantity** box, just click on the **Apply** button without making any changes.

7. Click on the arrow next to the filters **add** link and select **sort**. In the resulting window, drag the quantity field to be above the measure field, and click on the **Apply** button.

8. Click on the **Settings** link next to **Table** in the **Format** section, select **Right** for the **Align** setting for **Quantity**, and click on the **Apply** button.

9. Click on the **Save** button at the top of the page.

10. Across from the **Displays** list, click on the arrow next to **edit name and description** and select **Analyze**.

11. The results box should indicate that there is nothing to report. Click on the **Ok** button.

12. Navigate to /shopping-list to see the view:

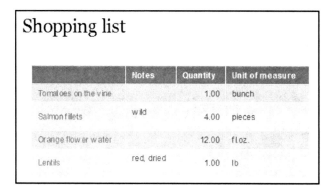

How it works...

The table format style exposes the view fields in HTML table format. Remember to select the fields, because the table format option cannot be saved unless at least one field has been selected for the view.

There's more...

We took the default options for the table style. One tremendous benefit of using this styling is that when editing the style options for the table, each of the field columns has a checkbox that, when checked, makes that column sortable by clicking on its title. For example, if you have a Price field in your data, and you set that checkbox for sortable, the column title Price will be a clickable link, which when clicked, will sort the data by price. We will do this in the next recipe.

Sortable table with a header and footer

It might seem like the only text in a view display can be the title, fields, and their headings, if any, but there is no such limitation. Two forms of text that can be added to views are a header and footer. We will create a view that uses both.

Getting ready

▸ This recipe uses a custom content type, **Product**, the details of which are in *Appendix B, Entity Types and Fields*.

▸ Create a few nodes of this content type

How to do it...

On the **Views List** page:

1. Navigate to the **Views List** page (`admin/structure/views`) and click on the **+Add new view** link.

2. Enter **Product list** as the **View title name**, check the box for **Description**, enter **A list of products for sale** as the **View description**, and click on the **Next** button. The **Show** options should be **Content**, **Product**, and **Title**.

3. In the **Display format**, select **Table** (the adjacent select boxes will disappear).

4. Click on the **Continue and edit** button.

   At this point, we have defined the overall view and now we can adjust its settings on the view edit page as follows.

5. Click on the **add** link next to **Fields**, check the boxes for **Fields: Body**, **Fields: Product image**, and **Fields: Product price**, and then click the **Add and configure** button.

6. In the **Configure field Fields: Body** box, select **Summary or Trimmed** in the **Formatter** select box, change **600** to **200** in **Trim length**, change the label to **Product description**, click on the **Rewrite Results** link, and check the box for **Strip HTML tags**. Then click on the **Apply and continue** button.

7. In the **Configure field Fields: Product image** box, clear the **Create a label** checkbox, select **thumbnail** from the **Image style** select box, and then click on the **Apply and continue** button.

8. In the **Configure field Fields: Product** price box, change the label to **Price**, then click on the **Apply** button.

9. Click on the link for **Content: Title** in the **Fields** section, check the box for **Create a link**, enter **Product** as the title, and then click on the **Apply** button.

10. Click on the arrow next to the filters **add** link and select **sort**. In the resulting window, drag the product image field to be above the title field, and click on the **Apply** button.

    So far, we have made general adjustments to the settings. Now we will do the things that make this recipe different from the previous one:

11. Click on the **Settings** link next to **Table** in the **Format** section, check the **Sortable** box for **Product** and for **Price**, click on the radio button to make **Product** the default sort item, select **Right** for the **Align** setting for **Price**, and click on the **Apply** button.

12. Click on the **add** link for **Header**, check the box for **Global: Text area**, then click on the **Add and configure** button.

13. Enter **<strong>Below is a list of all products currently for sale. Click on the column heading for Product or Price to sort the list based on that field. Click the column heading once will sort from lowest to highest. Click a second time will sort from highest to lowest. </strong>** as the header text and click on the **Apply** button.

14. Click on the **add** link for **Footer**, check the box for **Global: Text area**, then click on the **Add and configure** button.

15. Enter **<strong>Below is a list of all products currently for sale. Click on the column heading for Product or Price to sort the list based on that field. Click the column heading once will sort from lowest to highest. Click a second time will sort from highest to lowest. </strong>** as the header text and click on the **Apply** button.

16. Click on the **Save** button at the top of the page.

17. From the **Displays** list, click on the arrow next to **edit name and description** and select **Analyze**.

18. The results box should indicate that there is nothing to report. Click on the **OK** button.

19. Navigate to /product-list to see the view:

How it works...

Items in the table include a product image with a preset of thumbnails. We created a basic field-driven content view, and used a table for the display style: the size, the product name as a link to the node content, a trimmed version of the product description stripped of all HTML, and the product price. We reordered the fields to show the image first. We configured the table to sort initially by the product name, and made the product name and price columns selectable as sorting keys by clicking on the applicable column heading. We added a header with some formatting and a footer.

There's more...

The widget for creating a header or footer allows HTML to be entered, and, depending on the permissions granted by the admin, to select from a number of input formats. Thus, there are many possibilities, including having an image present with either. There is an option to show or suppress headers or footers if there is no content to show. There is also a way to use a view as the contents of the header or footer, for those cases where the text needs to be dynamic.

Using AJAX for page changes

In the normal scheme of things, changing pages with a pager results in the entire web page being reloaded. This can be annoying for the site visitor, particularly if the page loads result in advertisements being loaded from remote sites, which often causes a delay. Paging through 20 pages of output can be irksome, and more so if the paging is being done in a block rather than the main content area. Fortunately, there is a way to make the experience more enjoyable for the user, and that is by using AJAX for the page changes.

Getting ready

This recipe uses any node of any content type that defines **field_image** and contains an uploaded image.

How to do it...

On the **Views List** page:

1. Navigate to the **Views List** page (`admin/structure/views`) and click on the **+Add new view** link. Enter **Photo gallery** as the **View title name**, check the box for **Description**, enter **Gallery of images transitioned via AJAX** as the **View description**, and click on the **Next** button.

2. The **Show** options should be **Content, All,** and **Newest first**.

3. Clear the checkbox for **Create a page**.

4. Check the box for **Create a block**.

5. Change the selection in the **Display format** of the select box from **titles (linked)** to **fields**.

6. Change **Items per page** to **1**.

7. Click on the **Continue and edit** button.

   At this point, we have defined the overall view and now we can adjust its settings on the view edit page, as follows.

8. Click on the **add** button next to **Filter Criteria**, check the box for **Fields: Image (field_image) - fid,** and click on the **Add and configure filter criteria** button.

9. In the **Configure filter criterion** box, change **Operator** to **Is not empty (NOT NULL)** and click on the **Apply** button.

10. Click on the **add** link next to **Fields**, check the boxes for **Fields: Image**, and click on the **Add and configure** button.

11. In the configuration box, select the **Image style** of **thumbnail**, clear the **Create a label** checkbox, and click on the **Apply** button.

12. Click on the **Update** button.

13. If the advanced configuration items are hidden, click on the **Advanced** link to reveal them. Click on **No** next to **Use AJAX**, **Yes** in the configuration box, then click on the **Apply** button.

14. Click on **None** next to **Block name:** in the **Block settings** box. Enter **AJAX gallery** as the **Block admin description**, and click on the **Apply** button.

15. Click on the **Save** button.

16. Navigate to `admin/structure/block`, scroll down to the **AJAX gallery** listing, select a region for it to appear in (I used **Sidebar first**, but regions will vary from theme to theme), and click on the **Save blocks** button. Navigate to the home page to see the view. Using the pager to change the page will result in an AJAX page change, as shown in the following screenshot:

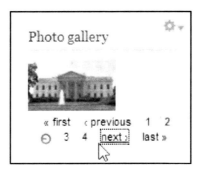

How it works...

We created a content view with a block display that selects any published node in which there is an uploaded image. We did this by specifying that the ID of **field_image** cannot be null. The field name could be different for you, based on the content type(s) you decide to use. We set the pager to allow one row per page, which means one image per page, as the image is the only field we will display. The key in this recipe is specifying the use of AJAX, which then uses that service to transit the images without reloading the page with each change.

Understanding relationships

A typical view will select information for each row from one data source, such as a node that meets the criteria of whatever filtering is in place. How do we handle a situation where the data for each row is *not* all in one place, where some of the data needs to come from another node? Enter the **relationship**, the widget in views that allows us to relate one data source to another. We will create a view that lists college courses from one content type, and draws the department name from another.

Getting ready

▸ This recipe uses two custom content types: **Course** and **Department**, the details of which are in *Appendix B, Entity Types and Fields*.

▸ Create a few nodes of each content type

How to do it...

On the **Views List** page:

1. Navigate to the **Views List** page (`admin/structure/views`) and click the **+Add new view** link, enter **Course list** as the **View name**, check the box for **Description**, enter **A list of courses** as the **View description**, and click the **Next** button. The **Show** options should be **Content**, **Course**, and **Title**.

2. In the **Page title** box, enter **Course list** in the **Display format** and select **Table** (the adjacent select boxes will disappear). **Click** on the **Continue and edit** button.

   At this point, we have defined the overall view, and now we can adjust its settings on the view's edit page.

3. Click the `Content: Title` link in the **Fields** section, change the **Label** from **Title** to **Course,** then click the **Update** button.

4. Click on the **add** link next to **Fields**, check the boxes for **Fields: Course credits** and **Fields: Course number**, and click on the **Add and configure fields** button.

5. In the **Configure field Fields: Course credits** overlay, click on the **Apply and continue** button.

6. In the **Configure field Fields: Course number** overlay, click the **Apply** button.

   Now we will create the relationship that links the selected Course node to a Department node.

7. Click the **Advanced** link to reveal the advanced settings.

8. Click the **add** link beside **Relationships**, check the box for **Fields: Department (field_department_ref) – nid,** and click the **Add and configure relationships** button. Then click the **Apply** button.

9. Click the **add** link next to **Fields**, check the box for **Content: Title**, and click the **Add and configure fields** button.

10. In the **Configure field Content: Title** overlay change the label from **Title** to **Department**, click the **More** link, change the **Relationship** setting to **field_department_ref**, and click the **Apply** button.

11. Click the `Settings` link in the **Format** section and click the radio button for **Default sort** for **Course**. Then, click the **Apply** button.

12. Click the None link for **Path** in the **Page Settings** section, change the path to **course-list**, and click the **Update** button.

13. Click the **Save** button at the top of the page.

14. Navigate to /course-list to see the view:

Course list

Course	Course credits	Course number	Department
Beginning Banjo	2	MU106	Music
Biology	4	SC101	Science
Biology Lab	2	SC102	Science
Business Management	3	BU101	Business
Early European History	3	HI101	History
English Composition	3	EN101	English
English Literature	3	EN102	English
Functions and Polynomials	3	MA101	Math
Fundamentals of Teaching	3	ED101	Education
Intro to Programming	2	CS101	Computer science

1 2 next › last »

How it works...

We created a node view that displays the fields in a specific content type, Course. We selected the table style to display the data. We wanted to display the department name along with the course, but the department name is contained in another content type Department rather than Course. The Course content type contains the field Department that holds a node reference, a pointer to the applicable Department node.

Therefore, we needed a way to access the content of the Department node that is referred to from the Course node, and we did that by establishing a relationship between the two. Then, when we chose the **Content: Title** field for the second time, we specified the field it uses in the relationship, giving it the Department title rather than the Course title.

There's more...

A relationship, in SQL parlance, is a *join*. Thus, when we establish a relationship between Course and Department using the department node reference (its nid) in the course node, the resulting SQL fragment would be as follows:

```
LEFT JOIN department ON department.nid = course.department_ref
```

In addition, the field that we display will be selected as **department.title** instead of **course. title**, because we identify it as using the department relationship. What this means is that we are not limited to one relationship, but can, if we need, have several.

Why use another content type?

Why do that instead of simply embedding the department name in the course record? Because if we did that, and the name of a department changes, we would need to change it in each course record for that department. So, why not define a select field in the course record, and enter the department names as the allowed values from which to choose? In this way, if the name of the department changes, it only has to be changed once, in the select's available values. This is because the field holds the select value index, which would remain the same. That would be acceptable, but our department content type contains the department phone number, Chairman's name, and degree programs, and not just the department name—information useful for other views—so all of that information would need to be duplicated as well.

Grouping in a query

If you are familiar with spreadsheets or reports, then you must be familiar with the concept of grouping and segregating data items by a higher-level value, such as students in a class. We will create a view that lists departments and the college courses within them.

Getting ready

- ▶ This recipe uses two custom content types: **Course** and **Department**, the details of which are in *Appendix B, Entity types and Fields*.
- ▶ Create a few nodes of each content type

How to do it...

On the **Views List** page:

1. Navigate to the **Views List** page (`admin/structure/views`) and click on the **+Add new view** link. Enter **department_Enter Department course_list** as the **View name**, check the box for **Description**, enter **A list of courses** as the **View description**, and click on the **Next** button.

2. The **Show** options should be **Content**, **Course**, and **Title**. In the **Page title** box, enter **Department course list**. In the **Display format**, select **Table** (the adjacent select boxes will disappear). Click on the **Continue and edit** button.

    At this point, we have defined the overall view and now we can adjust its settings on the view edit page, as follows.

3. Click on the **Content: Title** link in the **Fields** section, change the **Label** from **Title** to **Course**, and then click on the **Update** button.

4. Click on the **add** link next to **Fields**, check the boxes for **Fields: Course credits** and **Fields: Course number**, and then click on the **Add and configure fields** button.

5. In the **Configure field Fields: Course credits** overlay, click on the **Apply and continue** button.

6. In the **Configure field Fields: Course number** overlay, click on the **Apply** button.

    Now we will create the relationship that links the selected Course node to a Department node as follows.

7. Click on the **Advanced** link to reveal the advanced settings.

8. Click on the **add** link besides **Relationships**, check the box for **Fields: Department (field_department_ref) – nid**, and click on the **Add and configure relationships** button. Then click the **Apply** button.

9. Click on the **add** link next to **Fields**, check the box for **Content: Title**, and click the **Add and configure fields** button.

10. In the **Configure field Content: Title** overlay, change the label from **Title** to **Department**, check the box to **Exclude from display**, click on the **More** link, change the **Relationship** setting to **field_department_ref**, and click the **Apply** button.

11. Click the **Settings** link in the **Format** section and click the radio button for **Default sort** for the department field. Choose that same field for the **Grouping field**, and then click on the **Apply** button.

12. Click on the **None** link for **Path** in the **Page Settings** section, change the path to **department-course-list**, and click on the **Update** button.

13. Click on the **Save** button at the top of the page.

14. Navigate to `/department-course-list` to see the view:

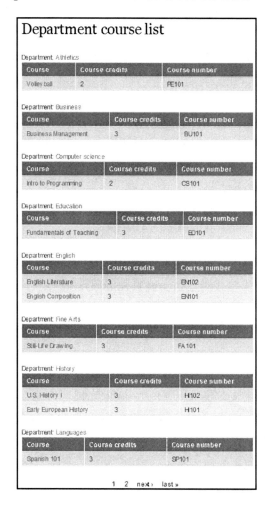

How it works...

We created a node view that displays the fields in two content types: Course and Department. We selected the table style to display the data. We wanted to display the department information along with the course, but the department name is contained in another content type. The Course content type contains a node reference to the applicable Department node, but the actual string containing the name of that department is not present in the Course content, but is the title of the Department node itself.

Therefore, we needed a way to access the content of the Department node that is referred to from the Course node, and we did that by establishing a relationship between the two. That would have simply given us a list of courses, but we wanted the list to be courses within each department, so we elected to *group* the records by department.

Nodes within nodes

We can think of catalogs, real estate listings and the like, as containers of similar content. For example, real estate listings may have some introductory text and other information that appears once within the page, and then a series of like-formatted home listings.

While we can replicate this with a view, the replication is not persistent, in terms of each page containing the same information reliably, and sometimes we need it to be. It is possible to do this by using a content type. The content type can contain the unique information, as well as node references and pointers, which point to the home listing data. This recipe allows us to create such a pairing.

Getting ready

▶ This recipe uses two custom content types: **Home and Real Estate flier**, the details of which are in *Appendix B, Entity Types and Fields*.

▶ Create some nodes of each content type

How to do it...

On the **Views List** page:

1. Navigate to the **Views List** page (`admin/structure/views`) and click the **+Add new view** link and click the **+Add new view** link. Enter **Real estate_ flier** as the **View title**, **name**, check the box for **Description**, enter **Weekly real estate deals** as the **View description**, and click on the **Next** button.

2. The **Show** options should be **Content**, **Real Estate flier**, and **Newest first**.

3. Change **teasers to fields** in **Display format**, and click on the **Continue and edit** button.

   At this point, we have defined the overall view and now we can adjust its settings on the view edit page as follows.

4. Click on the **add** link next to **Fields**, check the boxes for **Fields: Body** and **Fields: Property**, and click on the **Add and configure fields** button.

5. In the **Configure field Fields: Body** overlay, clear the **Create a label** checkbox and click on the **Apply and continue** button.

6. In the **Fields: Property** configuration box, clear the **Create a label** textbox, select **Rendered node** from the **Formatter** select box, and click on the **Apply** button.

7. Click on the **add** button in the **Header** box, check the box for **Global: Text area**, and click on the **Add and configure** button.

8. Enter **<h1>FIGMENT REALTY</h1>** in the textarea, select **Full HTML** from the **Text format** select box, and click on the **Apply** button.

9. Click on the **Save** button at the top of the page.

10. Navigate to /real-estate-flier to see the view:

FIGMENT REALTY

This Week's Hot Properties!
Labor Day usually marks the start of the market slowdown. Don't miss the best deals of the summer!

DH777777

237 rooms plus kitchens, maintenance, reception rooms and storage areas. All modern conveniences.

Zip code:
20006
Home image:

House price:
37 000 000.00
,

M999999

On 640 acres, with 43 rooms in 11,000 square feet. No indoor plumbing or central air.

Zip code:
229021234
Home image:

How it works...

We created a somewhat standard node view, except that the node content type that we selected, Real Estate flier, contains a field that itself contains multiple node references. This means that this field in the Real Estate flier contains an array of node IDs, each one being the ID of a node of the type Home. In this way, we created a flier that contains any number of real-estate entries, the inclusion of which is based solely on what we specifically desire to include, rather than selection criteria that can be expressed in a filter setting.

There's more...

We specified that the entire node should be displayed for each home. We could have specified that a teaser be shown instead. However, if we wanted to print the flier, each home would be a text excerpt with a "Read more" link, which would have little value in print. We could have created two displays: one for print and one for online, with the former showing the complete node and the latter a teaser.

Producing custom links

It is common to see a teaser for a node, a link as the title of the node, or an image link in the teaser, or a "Read more" link to the full node itself. This can be easily accomplished in a view by checking the box for **Link this field to its node** in the settings box for any field. Sometimes, though, we want to provide a link to a view instead of a node, or to a page callback for a custom module, or perhaps even to another site altogether. We will create a view that creates custom links.

Getting ready

This recipe uses the content types listed in *Appendix B, Entity Types and Fields*.

If you have not already done so, create a node for at least some of the content types

How to do it...

On the **Views List** page:

1. Navigate to the **Views List** page (`admin/structure/views`) and click on the **+Add new view** link. Enter **Custom node_links** as the **View title**, check the box for **Description**, enter **An index of site content, with each entry being a custom link** as the **View description**, and click on the **Next** button.

2. The **Show** options should be **Content**, **Real Estate flier**, and **Newest first**. Change **teasers to fields** in **Display format**. In the **Page** section, change **Display format** to **Unformatted list of Titles**, and click on the **Continue and edit** button.

At this point, we have defined the overall view and now we can adjust its settings on the view edit page as follows.

3. Click on the **add** button next to **Fields**, check the boxes for **Content: Nid** and **Content: Type**, and click on the **Add and configure fields** button.

4. In both configuration overlays, clear the **Link this field to the original piece of content** checkbox, the **Create a label** checkbox, check the **Exclude from display** checkbox, and click on the **Apply and continue** button.

5. Click on the arrow next to the **add** button in the **Fields** section and select **Sort**, drag the **Title** field to the bottom of the list, and click on the **Apply** button.

6. Click on the **Content: Title** field link, uncheck the **Link this field to the original piece of content** checkbox, click on the **Rewrite Results** link, and check the **Rewrite the output of this field** and **Output this field as a link** boxes.

7. In the textarea that appears, enter **[title] ([type] node: [nid])**.

8. In the **Link path** textbox, enter **myview/[nid]**, and then click on the **Apply** button.

9. Click on the **Save** button at the top of the page.

10. Navigate to **custom-node-links** to see the view:

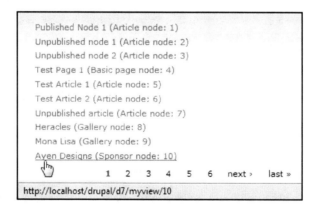

How it works...

We created a node view that selects all published nodes. We chose to include the fields for the `nid` and the `node type`, but specified that their value should not be displayed. The reason for this is that we wanted their values available to be used as replacement tags elsewhere.

We then reordered the fields, because replacement tags were not available to be used unless the field that they come from has already been defined. As we wanted both the `node type` and `nid` values available to the node title field, it had to come last.

Finally, we rewrote the output value of the title field to include the `node type` and `nid` in the link text, and changed the link value to point to a view, with the `nid` as an argument.

Proving a negative with a filter and an argument

In most of the content sites, the user will view only the published content. However, there is often unpublished content present; for example, the content that is in process, waiting to be edited, waiting for its date or season to come around, and so on.

Users with the permission to edit the content often get to it by navigating to that content's display and clicking on the **Edit** tab. If the content is unpublished, there is usually no way to get to it from the frontend; however, you can navigate to it from the admin content list.

It would be nice if users with permissions to create the content could access their own unpublished content in an easy manner, and they can! We will build a view that provides the user with a block that lists their unpublished content, and even allows them to filter dynamically on the content type.

Getting ready

- ▶ This recipe uses nodes of any content type, including those listed in *Appendix B, Entity Types and Fields*.

- ▶ Ensure that there are some unpublished nodes present

How to do it...

On the **Views List** page:

1. Navigate to the **Views List** page (`admin/structure/views`) and click on the **+Add new view** link. Enter **Unpublished content** as the **View name** and click on the **Next** button. The **Show** options should be **Content**, **All**, and **Newest first**. Clear the **Create a page** checkbox, check the **Create a block** box, and click on the **Continue and edit** button.

    At this point, we have defined the overall view and now we can adjust its settings on the view edit page, as follows.

2. Click on the **add** button next to **Fields**, check the boxes for **Content: Nid** and **Content: Type**, and click on the **Add and configure fields** button.

3. In both configuration overlays, clear the **Link this field to the original piece of content** checkbox, the **Create a label** checkbox, check the **Exclude from display** checkbox, and click on the **Apply and continue** button.

4. Click on the arrow next to the **add** button in the **Fields** section and select **Sort**, drag the **Title** field to the bottom of the list, and click on the **Apply** button.

5. Click on the **Content: Title** field link, uncheck the **Link this field to the original piece of content** checkbox, click on the **Rewrite Results** link, and check the **Rewrite the output of this field** and **Output this field as a link** boxes.

6. In the text area that appears, enter **[title] ([type] node: [nid])**.

7. In the **Link path** textbox, enter **myview/[nid]**, and then click on the **Apply** button.

8. Click on the **Save** button at the top of the page.

9. Navigate to **custom-node-links** to see the view.

10. Click on **None** next to **Block name**, in the **Block settings** box. Enter **Your unpublished content** in the textbox, and click on the **Apply** button.

11. Click on **Content: Published** in the **Filters** box. Change **Yes** to **No** and click on the **Apply** button. Click on the **+** icon in the **Filters** box, check the box next to **Node: Type**, the box next to **User: Current**, and click on the **Add and configure field criteria** button.

12. Check the button **Expose this filter**, the **Is one of** radio button, the **Select all** checkbox in **Content types**, the **operator** box **Remember selections** and **Allow multiple selections**, clear the **Force single** checkbox, and click on the **Apply** button.

13. Click on the **Yes** radio button for **Is the logged in user?** and click on the **Update** button.

14. Click on the **+** icon in the **Fields** box, check the box next to **Node: Edit link**, and click on the **Apply and configure fields** button.

15. Check the **Edit link** settings box, clear the checkbox for creating a label, click on the **Rewrite Results** link, check the **Rewrite the output of this field** box, enter **Edit** in the textbox that appears, check the **Output this field as a link** box, enter **[edit_node]** in the textbox that appears, and click on the **Apply** button.

16. Click on the **Settings** link next to **Fields** in the **Format** area, check both the **Inline fields** boxes, and click on the **Apply** button.

17. Click on the **Save** button.

18. Navigate to the blocks admin page (`admin/structure/block`), scroll down to **Your unpublished content** in the **Disabled** section, select a region for the block (I am using **Second sidebar)** from the select box, and click on the **Save blocks** button.

19. Navigate to the front page to view the block:

Unpublished content

Unpublished article (edit)
Unpublished node 2 (edit)
Unpublished node 1 (edit)

How it works...

We created a node view by adding a block display to an existing view, and set it to select the unpublished content. We added the content type as a filter with specific values selected, but exposed the filter for the user to make a selection. We also specified that the content must belong to the current user. The default setting for the title is to be a link to its content, and we added an edit link and specified its title. In this way, the user can select to click on the title and view the node, or click on the edit link and edit the node.

4
Creating Advanced Views

In this chapter, we will cover:

- Creating a view with multiple personalities
- Marketing bundle
- Filtering with 'or'
- Forming a dashboard with Page, Block, and Attachment displays
- Teaming two content lists
- Using related content: Adding depth to a term ID
- Using related content: Adding depth to a term
- Limiting visibility of content

Introduction

In this chapter, we will explore the capability of views that can provide multiple displays, sometimes simultaneously. Right out-of-the-box views can create page, block, attachment, and RSS displays, and with displays being pluggable, contributed modules can add to that list. This chapter introduces the basics of using multiple displays, with further capabilities using theming presented in *Chapter 5, Intermediate Custom Theming Views*. The book, *Drupal 6 Attachment Views*, by *Packt Publishing* delves further into this topic.

Creating a view with multiple personalities

It might seem that given the challenge of presenting different content types in different ways, there are two choices—create a separate view for each or write code in a module or template file. Depending on the need, the latter might be a reasonable option, but if all that is required are minor differences in node selection, sort order, or the fields to be presented, there is a better alternative available.

We are going to create a view, where most of the work is done in an umbrella fashion. That is, the core of the view will serve as a template. Then, we will create a display containing minor variances for each content type instead of having to create a view for each type.

Getting ready

We will be using the Blog entry and Home content types. Carry out the following steps in order to get started:

1. Enable the Blog module if you have not done so.
2. Refer to *Appendix B, Entity Types and Fields*, for details on the Home content type.
3. Create some entries for each content type.

How to do it...

Carry out the following steps in order to complete the recipe:

1. Navigate to the **Views List** page (`admin/structure/views`) and click on the **+Add** new view link. Enter **Chameleon** as the **View name**, check the box for **Description**, enter **View title and Content type displays** as the **View description**, and click on the **Next** button.
2. The **Show** options should be **Content**, **All**, and **Title**.
3. In the **Create a page** section, change the **Page** title from **Chameleon** to **Blog entries**, and the **Path** to **content/blog-entries**.
4. In the **Display** format change **Teasers** to **Titles (linked)** (the adjacent select boxes will disappear).
5. Click on the **Continue and edit** button.

At this point we have defined most of the information for one display, and now we can adjust its settings on the **View Edit** page:

1. Click on the **Page** link next to the **Display** name and change the name to **Blogs**. Then click on the **Apply** button.
2. Click on the **Add** link next to **Fields**, check the boxes for **Content: Post date**, and click on the **Add and configure** button.

3. In the **Configure field Content: Post date** box, change the label from **Post date** to **Posted**, and then click on the **Apply** button.

4. Click on the **Settings** link next to **Fields** in the **Format** section, check the box for each field listed beneath the **Inline** fields, and click on the **Apply** button.

5. Click on the **Add** link in the **Sort Criteria** section, check the box for **Content: Post date,** and click on the **Add and configure sort criteria** button. Select **Sort descending** and click on the **Apply** button. Click on the arrow next to **Sort Criteria add link** and select **Sort** in the resulting window. Drag the **Content: Title** field to be below **Content: Post date** and click on the **Apply** button.

6. Click on the **Add** link in the **Filters** section. Check the box for **Content: Type** and click on the **Add and configure filter criteria** button.

7. Check the box for **Content: type** and click on the **Apply** button.

8. That completes the **Blog** display, but this view will have more than one display. Now we will create the Homes display.

9. Click on the **Add page** button next to the **Page** button in the **Displays** section at the top.

10. Click on the **Page** link next to **Display name** and change the name to **Homes**. Then click on the **Apply** button.

11. Click **Blog entries** next to **Title**, change **All displays** to **This page (override)**, enter **Homes** as the title, and click on the **Apply** button.

12. Click **blog-entries** next to **Path:** in the **Page settings** box. Enter **content/homes** as the path, and click on the **Update** button.

13. Click on the **Content type (=Blog entry)** link in the **Filters** section, change **All displays** to **This page** (override), uncheck the box for **Blog entry**, check the box for **Home**, and click on the **Apply** button.

14. Click on the **Content: Post date** link in the **Fields** section, change the select box to **This display (override)** and click on the **Remove** button.

15. Click on the **add** link in the **Fields** box, check the boxes for **Fields: Image** and **Fields: Price**, and click on the **Apply and continue** button.

16. Change the select box setting to **This display (override)**, clear the **Create a label** checkbox, select **Content** from the **Link image to** select box, **medium** from the **Formatter** select box, and click on the **Apply and continue** button.

17. Clear the checkbox for **Create a label**, change the **Thousand** marker to **Comma, the Scale** from **2** to **0**, and click on the **Apply** button.

18. Click on the **add** link in the **Sort criteria** box, check the box next to the **Fields: Product** price, and click on the **Apply and configure sort criteria** button. Change the override setting to **This display (override)** and click on the **Apply** button.

19. Click on the other two sort field links and then their **Remove** buttons.

20. Click on the **Save** button at the top of the page.

21. Navigate to the `/content/blog-entries` to see the following screenshot:

Blog entries

We need another blog entry Posted: Sun, 09/05/2010 - 21:24
Chocolate is the New Black of Food Posted: Fri, 08/13/2010 - 23:43

22. Navigate to the `/content/homes` to see the following screenshot:

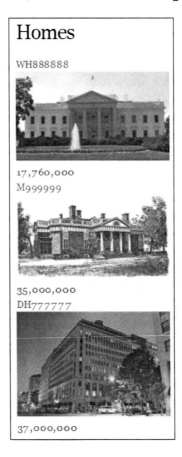

How it works...

We created a content view, and then created two page displays within it, one for each of the blog entry and home content types. Each display has its own filters, sort criteria, field selection, and title.

There's more...

There is more than one way to accomplish the results we see here. We could have created a template for each node type, and one view display that selects records based on an argument. Templates are discussed in the next chapter. The decision should be based on whether there are likely to be changes to the view later on, and who is going to be maintaining it; if a developer or themer will be maintaining it, then perhaps a template is the way to go, but if an editor with little or no programming experience is going to do so, then this method could be better.

A variation on this would be to create each display as a block instead of a page, and to assign each to the content area on the front page. If you are doing so, and if you are using a pager for each, remember that every pager must have its own ID number, so be sure to change the pager number setting for each.

Marketing bundle

Each view's display type has its own strengths. They can be combined in different ways to create a set of related displays to fulfill a single purpose. In this recipe, we will create a **marketing bundle**. We will use a page display for a sales presence landing page, a block display for an ad, and an RSS feed with which customers can stay updated about new content.

Getting ready

We will be using the Product content type (refer to *Appendix B, Entity Types and Fields*, for details). At least one product node will be needed in order to get started with the recipe.

How to do it...

Carry out the following steps in order to complete this recipe:

1. Navigate to the **Views List** page (`admin/structure/views`) and click on the **+Add new view** link.

2. We will first enter some settings to create a page. Enter **Marketing bundle** as the **View name**, check the box for **Description**, enter **Landing page, ad and RSS feed** as the **View description**. The **Show** options should be **Content**, **Product**, and **Title**. In the **Page title** box enter **Greenberg Design Accessories U.S. Brings You the Best Bargains!**. Enter **bargains** in the **Path** box. For **Display format** select **Grid**, and **Fields** (the other two select boxes will disappear). Change the **Items per page** to **3**.

3. Next, we will enter the settings to create a block. Check the box for **Create a block**. For the block title enter **Another Great Greenberg Design Accessories U.S. Product**. Change **titles (linked)** to **fields** in **Display format** and **Items per page** to **1**. Click on the **Continue and edit** button.

At this point we have defined the overall view, and now we can adjust its settings on the view edit page:

1. Click on the **Settings** link next to **Grid** and change **Columns** from **4** to **3**. Click on the **add** link next to **Fields**, check the boxes for **Content: Product image** and click on the **Add and configure** button. In the **Configure field Fields: Product** image box, change the **For select** box from **All displays** to **This page (override)**, clear the **Create a label** checkbox, select **medium** from the **Image style** select box, select **Content** in the **Link image to** select box, then click on the **Apply and continue** button.

2. Click on the link for **Content: Title** in the **Fields** section, clear the box for **Create a link**, click on the **Rewrite Results** link to open the dialog, check the box for **Rewrite the output of this field**, enter **<h2>[title]</h2>** in the text box, then click on the **Apply** button.

3. Click on the **add** link in the **Header** box. click on the **Global: Text area** checkbox, click on the **Add and configure** button, change the setting in the **For** box from **All displays** to **This page (override)**, enter **<big>The liquidation area of Greenberg Design Accessories U.S. is where you can find amazing bargains in leftover and discontinued products.</big>** in the large text box, select **Full HTML** from the **Text format** select box, and click on the **Apply** button.

4. Click on the **add** link in the **Footer** box, click on the **Global: Text area** checkbox in the settings box that opens, click on the **Add and configure** button, change the setting in the **For** box from **All displays** to **This page (override)**, enter **<small>Greenberg Design Accessories U.S. is a division of Acme Holding Corp</small>** in the large text box, select **Full HTML** from the **Text format** select box, and click on the **Apply** button.

That takes care of the page display. Next we will make further adjustments to the block display:

1. Click on the **Block** button in the **Displays** section. Click on the link for **Post date** in the **Sort criteria** box, change the select box from **All displays** to **This block (override)** , and click on the **Remove** button.

2. Click on the **add** link in the **Sort criteria** box, check the box for **Global: Random**, click on the **Add and configure sort criteria** button, change the select box setting from **All displays** to **This block (override),** and click on the **Apply** button.

3. Click on the **Content: Title** link in the **Fields** section, change the select box setting to **This block (override),** and click on the **Remove** button.

4. Click on the **Content: Product image** link in the **Fields** section, change the select box setting to **This block (override)**, change the **Image style** to **Thumbnail**, and click on the **Apply** button.

5. The final step is to create the RSS feed.

6. Click on the **+Add** button in the **Displays** section and click on the **Feed** link. Click **None** next to **Path:** in the **Feed settings** box, enter **greenbergdesignaccessories/ feed** as the path, and click on the **Apply** button.

7. Click on the title in the **Title** box, change the select box setting to **This feed (override)**, enter **The Newest Bargains from Greenberg Design Accessories U.S.** in the text box, and click on the **Apply** button.

8. Click on the **Settings** link next to **RSS Feed** in the **Format** section, select **Title** only from the **Display type** select box, and click on the **Apply** button.

9. Click on the **Global: Random** link next to **Sort criteria**, change the select box setting to **This feed (override)**, and click on the **Remove** button.

10. Click on the **add** link for **Sort Criteria**, check the box for **Content: Post date**, and click on the **Add and configure sort criteria** button. Change the select box setting to **This feed (override)** and choose **Sort descending**.

11. Click on the **Save** button.

12. Navigate to the **Block Admin** page (`admin/structure/block`), find **Marketing bundle ad** in the **Disabled** section, and change the select box setting to **Sidebar first**. Then click on the **Save** blocks button.

13. Navigate to the home page to see the block shown in the following screenshot:

14. Navigate to the RSS feed (`greenbergdesignaccessories/feed`), which appears as shown in the following screenshot:

15. Navigate to the landing page (`bargains`), which appears as in the following screenshot:

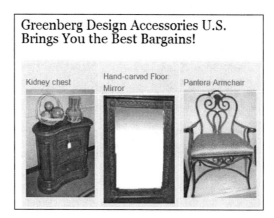

How it works...

We created a node view that selects nodes of the Product content type. We then built three displays, a block that can be used as an advertisement, a RSS feed that can be used to allows users to subscribe and keep current with the site, and a landing page that can be used, for example, when the user clicks on an ad on another site. The main idea behind this view is that each display can have its own settings with regards to fields, sort criteria, and even the filter settings, though we used the same filter throughout this example.

Filtering with 'or'

Filtering is the way to control record selection in a view, whether through contextual filters or regular filters (there is no contrasting term for the latter, but when they are exposed for the user to choose a filtering value, they, too, become contextual).

It is possible, and typical, to use two or more filters in conjunction, such as requiring that content be a specific type and be published, or more precisely, that content be of a certain type and be published. When the two filters are put into effect, if either requirement is not met, the content will not be selected. Hence, if the content is published but is the wrong type, or is the correct type but is unpublished, it will not be selected. This is fine, if it is the requirement.

Let us use an analogy: *buying shoes*. Filtering such as this is the equivalent of asking the sales clerk for shoes that are *size 8 and casual and leather*. You want all three requirements to be met. However, you could also ask for shoes that are *size 8 and are either casual or leather*. In other words, they must be your size, but aside from that, they will be acceptable if they are casual, leather, or both.

In the previous example, the requirements can be written as:

```
size = 8 and (style = casual or material = leather)
```

In prior versions of views, having 'or' filters was problematic, at best, but *Views 3* makes it easy, and in this recipe we will create a view that uses them.

Getting ready

The following will be needed for this recipe:

1. One node of the Ingredient content type (refer to *Appendix B, Entity Types and Fields*, for details).

2. One node of a different content type, with the word 'food' somewhere in the content or title.

How to do it...

On the **View List** page carry out the following steps in order to complete this recipe:

1. Navigate to the **Views List** page (`admin/structure/views`) and click on the **+Add new view** link. Enter **Food topics** as the **View name**, check the box for **Description**, enter **Content that is a recipe or has 'food' in the title** as the **View description**, and click on the **Next** button. The **Show** options should be **Content**, **All**, and **Title**.

2. In the **Create a page** section, on the **Display format** line, change the **without comments** to **with comments**. Check the box for **Include an RSS feed**, and change the path from **food-topics.xml** to **food-topics/feed**. Click on the **Continue and edit** button.

At this point we have defined most of the information for one display, and now we can adjust its settings on the **View Edit** page:

1. Click on the **add** link in the **Filters** section, check the box for **Content: Title, Content: Type, Fields: Body (body) - value,** and click on the **Add and configure filter criteria** button.

2. In the **Content: Title configuration** dialog, change the **Operator selection** to **Contains**, enter **Food** in the **Value** textbox, and click on the **Apply and continue** button.

3. In the **Content: Type configuration** dialog check the box for the **Ingredient content type**, then click on the **Apply and continue** button.

4. In the **Field: Body configuration** dialog, change the **Operator selection** to **Contains**, enter **Food** in the **Value** textbox, and click on the **Apply** button.

5. Click on the down arrow next to the **add** link in the **Filter Criteria** section, and click on the **and/or** link.

6. Click on the **+ Create new filter group** link and drag the criteria aside from the one for **Content: Published** to the next group at the bottom. Change the lower operator to **Or**, and then click on the **Apply** button.

7. Click on the **Save** button at the top of the page.

8. Now, navigate to the food-topics page to see the following screenshot:

9. Navigate to the `food-topics/feed` to see the following screenshot:

How it works...

We accomplished two things in this recipe, the creation of a compound filter and a feed. We changed the path of the feed only for personal preference; the original path would have been fine.

We created the compound filter to accommodate **all/any logic**, where connecting rules with 'or' is the same as stating that 'any' of them can be true, while connecting them with 'and' is the same as stating that 'all' of them must be true. We put the filters in two groups, with 'and' between them, resulting in the following rule:

> ▸ Published AND (Ingredient node OR title contains 'food' OR body contains 'food')

Another way of reading this is:

> ▸ Content must be published, and one or more of the conditions (type=ingredient, body contains 'food', title contains 'food') must be true.

Forming a dashboard with Page, Block, and Attachment displays

You have probably used desktop applications where the screen is divided into two or more areas, each of them working in conjunction with the other. It is possible to achieve the same functionality on your web page. We will use a page display and attachment display, arguments, and relationships to create sections that work together to give more form and function to a view.

Getting ready

We will be using the Employee and Extension content types (refer to *Appendix B, Entity Types and Fields*, for details). Create at least two of each to get started with the recipe.

How to do it...

On the **View List** page, carry out the following steps in order to complete this recipe:

1. Navigate to the **Views List** page (`admin/structure/views`) and click on the **+Add new view** link.

2. We will first enter the settings to create a page:

   Enter **Employee extensions** as the **View name**, check the box for **Description**, enter **Employee information and extensions** as the **View description**. Change the entry in the **Path** box to **employees**. For **Display format** change **Teasers** to **Fields** (the other two select boxes will disappear). Click on the **Continue and edit** button.

At this point let's complete the page, which will display the employee information:

1. Click on the **add** link next to **Fields**, check the boxes for **Content: Department** (there are two; select the one that appears in employee content type), **Content: Employee ID**, and **Content: Position**, and click on the **Add and configure** button.

2. For each of the configured boxes that follow for each of the three fields, simply click on the **Apply and continue** button for the first two, and the **Apply** button for the third.

3. Click on the link for **Content: Title** in the **Fields** section, clear the box for **Link this field to the original piece of content**, click on the **Rewrite Results** link to open the dialog, check the box for **Rewrite the output of this field**, enter **<h2>[title]</h2>** in the text box, and then click on the **Apply** button.

4. Click on the **add** link for **Filter Criteria**, check the box for **Content: Type**, click on the **Add and configure filter criteria** button, check the box for **Employee**, and click on the **Apply** button.

5. Click on the **Advanced** link to reveal the advanced criteria.

6. Click on the **add** link for **Contextual Filters**, check the boxes for **Fields: Department (field_employee_dept) – value** and **Fields: Employee ID (field_employee_id) – value**, and click on the **Add and configure contextual filters** button.

7. Select **This page** at the top of the first configuration box that appears, and click on the **Apply and continue** button.

8. On the second configuration box that appears click on the **Apply** button.

9. Click on the **add** link for **Relationships**, check the box for **Fields: Extension (field_extension) – nid**, and click on the **Add and configure** relationships button.

10. In the subsequent configuration screen change the selection in the **For** select box to **This page (override)**, then click on the **Apply** button.

11. Click on the **add** link for **Fields** again, check the box for **Content: Extension**, and click on the **Apply and configure** button.

12. Change the **Relationship** selection from **Do not use a relationship to field_extension**, change the **Formatter setting** to **Title (no link)** and click on the **Apply** button.

That takes care of the page display. Next, we will create the block display that will display the departments:

1. Check the button to **+Add** a display and select **Block**. Click **None** next to **Title**, ensure that **This block (override)** is selected in the **For** select box, and click on the **Apply** button.

2. Click on the **add** link next to **Fields**, check the boxes for **Content: Department** and **Content: Title**, and click on the **Add and configure fields** button. In the configuration box for **Content: Department**, uncheck the **Create a label** checkbox, check the box for **Exclude from display**, and click on the **Apply and continue** button.

3. In the configuration box that follows, select **This block** from the select box at the top, uncheck both the **Create a label** and the **Link this field to the original piece of content** checkboxes, click on the **Rewrite Results** link, and check the box for Output this field as a link. Enter **employee/[field_employee_dept]** as the path, and click on the **Apply** button.

4. Click on the **add** link for **Filter Criteria**, check the box for **Content: Type**, click on the **Add and configure filter criteria** button, check the box for **Department**, and click on the **Apply** button.

The final step is to create the Attachment display that lists employees:

1. Click on the **+Add** button in the **Displays** section and click on the **Attachment** link.

2. Click on the **add** link next to **Fields**, check the boxes for **Content: Employee ID** and **Content: Title**, and click on the **Add and configure fields** button.

3. Click on the **Not defined** link for **Attach to** in the **Attachment Settings** box, select **Page**, and click on the **Apply** button.

4. In the configuration box for **Content: Employee ID**, uncheck the **Create a label** checkbox, check the box for **Exclude from display**, and click on the **Apply and continue** button.

5. In the configuration box that follows, select **This block** from the select box at the top, and uncheck both the **Create a label** and the **Link this field to the original piece of content** checkboxes.

6. Click on the **Rewrite Results** link and check the box for **Output this field as a link**. Enter **employee/all/[field_employee_id]** and click on the **Apply** button.

7. Click on the **add** link for **Sort Criteria**, check the box for **Content: Title**, and click on the **Add and configure sort criteria** button.

8. Change the select box setting to **This attachment (override)** and click on the **Apply** button.

9. Click on the **Save** button.

10. Navigate to the **Block Admin** page (**Admin | Structure | Block**), find **employee_ extensions** in the **Disabled** section, and change the select box setting to **Sidebar first**. Then click on the **Save blocks** button.

11. Click on the **Configure** link, and in the section for **Show block on specific pages**, select **Only the listed pages** and enter **employee*** in the textbox.

12. Navigate to /employee to see the components that we have created (this is the page which displays employee information). It will look like the following screenshot:

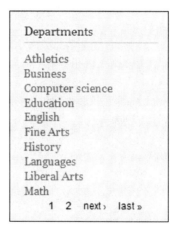

The block, which displays a list of departments, looks similar to the following screenshot:

The attachment, which displays a list of employees, looks similar to the following screenshot:

How it works...

You could very well be wondering about the application of this recipe until you give it a closer look. If you hover the mouse over a link in the **Department** list, and then a link in the **Employee** list, you will see that both link to the employee path, with a slight difference, which is that the department link will be of the form of employee/department, while the employee link will be of the form employee/all/employee.

There are a few things going on in this view that are worth mentioning. The page display determines which employee's information should be included in the list based on the arguments passed in the URL. The first argument specifies which department the employee(s) should be part of, or all, which means all values will be used. The second argument specifies the employee ID, or, if it is not present, all employees. We set the configuration of the department title and employee name to be a link back to the employee page with the appropriate arguments, so that when a department name or employee name are clicked, the page display of our view is invoked with the applicable arguments.

The other item worth noting is the employee extension. It is actually a separate content type, and so a separate table in the database. So, we retrieved the extension by establishing a relationship between the employee table and the extension table, which in turn creates a table join in the query.

There's more...

There are two further things that should be done to this view. It certainly needs formatting, and in this case view templates would probably be the ideal choice. Also, it is likely that this view should be restricted, so it should be determined which role(s) will be enabled to view its content.

Teaming two content lists

Sometimes you might want to split one set of records into two different displays; for example, a list of contacts where business contacts appear in one display and personal contacts in another. There is a trick for doing that and not having the same content in both. In this recipe, we will create a top ten list, but have the top three in one display and the remaining in another display.

Getting ready

We will be using the Country content type (refer to *Appendix B, Entity Types and Fields*, for details) in order to get started with the recipe.

How to do it...

On the **View List** page, carry out the following steps in order to complete this recipe:

1. Navigate to the **Views List** page (`admin/structure/views`) and click on the **+Add new view** link.

We will first enter the settings to create a page:

1. Enter **Top 10** as the **View name**, check the box for **Description**, and enter **Top 10 Country list** as the **View description**. Change the **Show type** to **Country**. Change the entry in the **Path** box to **top-10**. For **Display format** change **Teasers** to **Titles** (the other two select boxes will disappear). Click on the **Continue and edit** button.

2. Click on the link for **Content: Title**, select **This page (override)**, click on the link for **Style Settings**, check the box for **Wrap field in HTML**, change the **HTML element** to **H2**, and click on the **Apply** button.

3. Click on the link for **Post date** under **Sort criteria** and then the **Remove** button.

4. Click on the **add** link in **Sort criteria**, check the box for **Fields: Area (field_country_area)**, and click on the **Add and configure sort criteria** button.

5. Select **Sort descending** and click on the **Apply** button. Click on the link for **Use pager**, change the setting to **Display a specified number of records,** and click on the **Apply** button.

6. Change the number of **Records to display** to **3** and click on the **Apply** button.

That takes care of the page display. Next, we will create the attachment display:

1. Check the button to **+Add** a display and select **Attachment**. Click on the **10 items** link for **Items to display** in the **Pager** section. Change **Items to display** to **7** and **Offset** to **3**, then click on the **Apply** button. Click on the **Not defined** link for **Attach to** in the **Attachment settings** box, check the box for **Page**, then click on the link for **Before**, and change it to **After**. Then click on the **Apply** button.

2. Click on the **Save** button.

3. Navigate to /top-10 and you will see the following screen:

How it works...

The key to this recipe is the ability to specify an offset. For example, suppose you have content that is artwork and you have a place on the home page where you always display the most recent piece. On another page, you want to display other pieces, but not the one that is showcased on the home page. In that case, the selection would be given an offset of 1, presuming that the sort order is the same for both selections, otherwise an offset is meaningless.

The reason we made the appearance of the text for the top three different than that of the others was merely to provide a visual cue. Normally, CSS would be used to provide a demarcation between the two displays, and is beyond the scope of this recipe. If there were no differences in the appearance of the text, then the two lists—top three items and the remaining seven items—would have looked like just one list of 10 entries.

Using related content: Adding depth to a term ID

Give your visitors a useful site and they will come back. One thing that makes a content site more useful is providing the user with bonus content that is related to the content being viewed. In this recipe, we will create a display that shows a piece of content, and an attachment display that presents a list of links for related content.

Getting ready

We will be using the article content type in order to get started with the recipe. You need to do the following in order to get started with the recipe:

1. Create the taxonomy terms for this recipe, as shown in *Appendix B, Entity Types and Fields*.
2. Create a small article for each of the terms.

How to do it...

On the **Views List** page carry out the following steps in order to complete this recipe:

1. Navigate to the views list (**Admin | Structure | Views**) and click on the **+Add new view** link. Enter **Related content** as the **View name**, check the box for **Description**, enter **Use term ID** and depth to provide related content as the **View description**. Change the **Show type** to **Article**, **Teasers** to **Full node**, **Items per page** to **1**, and click on the **Continue and edit** button.

On the **View Edit** page:

1. Click on **Related content** next to **Title**, clear the textbox and click on the **Apply** button.

2. Click on the link for **Post date** under **Sort criteria** and then click on the **Remove** button.

3. Click on the **Advanced** link to reveal the advanced settings.

4. Click on the **add** button for **Contextual filters**, check the box for **Content: Nid,** and click on the **Add and configure contextual filters** button.

5. Select **This page (override)** from the select box and click on the **Apply** button.

That takes care of the page display. Next, we will create the attachment display:

1. Check the button to **+Add** a display and select **Attachment**.

2. Click on the link for **Post date** under **Sort criteria** and then the **Remove** button.

3. Click on the **Advanced** link to reveal the advanced settings.

4. Click on the **add** button for **Contextual filters**, check the boxes for **Global: Null** and **Taxonomy: Term ID (with depth)**, then click on the **Add and configure contextual filters** button.

5. In the configure box for **Global: Null**, select **This attachment (override)** from the select box, and click on the **Apply** button.

6. In the configure box for **Taxonomy: Term ID (with depth)** select a depth of **2** and click on the **Apply** button.

7. Click on the **Not defined** link for **Attach to** in the **Attachment settings** box, check the box for **Page**, then click on the link for **Before** and change it to **After** and click on the **Apply** button.

8. Click **Before** next to **Attachment position** in **Attachment settings**, select **After** instead of **Before**, and click on the **Apply** button.

9. The URL for this view will contain two arguments, the `nid` of the content to display and the `tid` (term ID) of the term to relate content to. In my case, the URL is `related-content/92/24`; yours can be different.

What NID and TID do I use?

The easiest way to determine a node's ID (nid) or term's ID (tid) is to go to the admin screen that lists nodes (`admin/content`) or terms (`admin/structure/taxonomy/your_vocabulary_name`), find the node or term, hover your mouse over its edit link, and look at the URL that appears at the bottom left of the screen for the number.

The Tourist Life

There are many things one needs to know in order to get the most
out of a vacation to a foreign destination. Here are some resources:

Tags:
Tourist Info

Lodging
Efficient Sightseeing
Where to Eat?
Joining the Group
The Tourist Life

How it works...

The secrets of this recipe are inherited arguments (contextual filters) and taxonomy
term depth.

The contextual filter defined in the page display is then passed to the attachment display.
However, we do not want to use that argument, because we will not be retrieving content
based on the `nid` (node ID) in the attachment, but we will be retrieving content based on the
`tid` (term ID). So, we have to do something with that argument so that it will not be used. It's
going to be in the URL, but we can 'tell' the attachment that the argument is something other
than it really is, and what we have told the attachment is that the argument is null, and thus it
is ignored.

The second argument is the term ID. You might notice that we have not defined a second
argument on the page display. Drupal allows you to put as much extra information in the URL
as you would like, and any arguments that are not defined are merely passed on and ignored.
So, the second argument is passed to the attachment without the page caring about it.

If we were to merely retrieve content that had the same `tid` as the node we requested, we
would only have that node to show (or others with the same tag, if any). However, our contextual
filter allowed us to define depth. We could have defined it as 0, meaning leave the choice as
the `tid` that was supplied as an argument. We could also have defined it as negative, so that
-1 would include the term's parent, -2 its grandparent, and so on. We defined it as 2, so that
children and grandchildren terms would be included.

Using related content: Adding depth to a term

This recipe is almost identical to the previous one, with an interesting twist. We are going
to force views to allow us to specify the desired content by providing a taxonomy term, as
opposed to the term's ID. If you have done the preceding recipe then you can jump right into
the *How to do it...* section.

Getting ready

We will be using the Article content type. Carry out the following steps in order to get started:

1. Create the taxonomy terms for this recipe, as shown in *Appendix B, Entity Types and Fields*.

2. Create a small article for each of the terms.

How to do it...

On the **View List** page carry out the following steps in order to complete this recipe:

1. Navigate to the views list (`admin/structure/views`) and click on the **+Add new view** link. Enter **Related content 2** as the **View name**, check the box for **Description**, and enter **Use term ID and depth to provide related content** as the **View description**. Change the **Show type** to **Article**, **Teasers** to **Full node**, **Items per page** to **1**, and click on the **Continue and edit button**.

On the view edit page:

1. Click **Related content** next to **Title**, clear the text box and click on the **Apply** button.

2. Click on the link for **Post date** under **Sort criteria** and then click on the **Remove** button.

3. Click on the **Advanced** link to reveal the **advanced** settings.

4. Click on the **add** button for **Contextual filters**, check the box for **Content: Nid,** and click on the **Add and configure contextual filters** button.

5. Select **This page (override)** from the select box and click on the **Apply** button.

That takes care of the Page display. Next we will create the Attachment display:

1. Check the button to **+Add** a display and select **Attachment**.

2. Click on the link for **Post date** under **Sort criteria** and then the **Remove** button.

3. Click on the **Advanced** link to reveal the advanced settings.

4. Click on the **add** button for **Contextual filters**, check the boxes for **Global: Null, Taxonomy: Term ID (with depth)**, and **Taxonomy: Term ID depth modifier**, then click on the **Add and configure contextual filters** button.

5. In the configure box for **Global: Null**, select **This attachment (override)** from the select box, and click on the **Apply** button.

6. In the configure box for **Taxonomy: Term ID (with depth),** select a depth of **0** and click on the **Apply** button.

7. In the configure box for **Taxonomy: Term Depth** click on the **Apply** button.

8. Click on the **Not defined** link for **Attach to** in the **Attachment settings** box, check the box for **Page**, then click on the link for **Before** and change it to **After** and click on the **Apply** button.

9. Click **Before** next to **Attachment position** in attachment settings, select **After** instead of **Before**, and click on the **Apply** button.

10. The URL for this view will contain three arguments, the `nid` of the content to display, the `tid` of the term to relate content to, and the amount of generations preceding the term (negative) or following the term (positive) to include. In my case the URL is `related-content2/98/21/-1`; yours is likely to be different. The following screen will appear:

Joining the Group

This is an article related to the Group Tours tag

Tags:
Group Tours

Efficient Sightseeing
Joining the Group

How it works...

The secrets of this recipe are inherited arguments (contextual filters) and taxonomy term depth modifier.

The contextual filter defined in the page display is then passed to the attachment display. However, we do not want to use that argument, because we will not be retrieving content based on the `nid` in the attachment, we will be retrieving content based on `tid`. Hence, we have to do something with that argument so that it will not be used. It's going to be in the URL, but we can tell the attachment that it is something other than it is, and what we told the attachment is that the argument is null, and thus it is ignored.

The second argument is the term ID. You might notice that we have not defined a second argument on the page display. Drupal allows you to put as much extra information in the URL as you would like, and any arguments that are not defined are merely passed on and ignored. So, the second argument is passed to the attachment without the page caring about it.

The third argument is a modifier, to change the depth setting for selecting taxonomy terms. We could have defined it as 0, meaning leave the choice as whichever `tid` we supplied as an argument. However, we defined it as -1, so that the term's parent is included.

Limiting visibility of content

In this recipe, we're going to create a block that lists the titles of content created by the current user, and a main display to allow viewing selected content. An example of the usage for this is similar to a site where each user has their own page, like on Facebook.

How to do it...

On the **View List** page carry out the following steps in order to complete this recipe:

1. Navigate to the views list (`admin/structure/views`) and click on the **+Add** new view link. Enter **Limited visibility** as the **View name**, check the box for **Description**, and enter **Present the user's content** as the **View description**. The **Show** options should be **Content and Article**. For **Display format**, select **Unformatted list** and **full posts, without links**, and **without comments**.

2. Next, we will enter the settings to create a block. Check the box for **Create a block**, and click on the **Continue and edit** button.

At this point we have defined the overall view, and now we can adjust its settings on the **View Edit** page:

1. Click on the **Advanced** link to reveal the advanced settings.

2. Click on the **add** button for **Contextual filters**, check the box for **Content: Nid**, and then click on the **Add and configure contextual filters** button.

3. In the configure box, select **This block (override)** from the select box and click on the **Apply** button.

That takes care of the page display. Next, we will make further adjustments to the Block display:

1. Click on the **Block** button in the **Displays** section. Click on the add link for **Fields**, check the box for **Content: Nid,** and click on the **Apply and configure fields** button.

2. In the **Content: Nid** configuration box, clear the checkbox for the label, check the box to exclude it from display, and click on the **Apply** button.

3. Click on the arrow next to the **Add** button in **Fields** and select **Sort**. Then rearrange the fields to put Nid first.

4. Click on the link for **Content: Title**, clear the **Label** textbox and the box for **Output this field as a link**, click on the link to **Rewrite output**, check the box of **Output the field as a link**, enter `limited-visibility/[nid]` in the **Link path** textbox, and click on the **Update** button.

5. Click on the **add** link for **Filters**, check the box for **User: Current**, and click **Add and configure** filters. Select **Is the current user** and click **Apply**.

6. Save the view.

7. Navigate to the **Block Admin** page (`admin/structure/block`), find **limited_visibility: Block** in the **Disabled** section, and change the select box setting to **Sidebar first**. Then click on the **Save blocks** button.

8. Navigate to the home page to see the block shown in the following screenshot. Clicking any link will display that content:

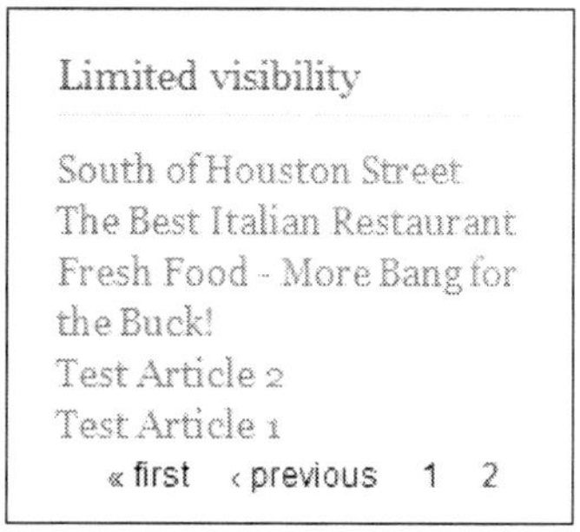

How it works...

We created a block display that creates a list of titles of the content created by the current user and displays those titles as links to a path with an argument of the ID of that content.

Next, we created a page display that will present a piece of content based on the ID that is passed in the URL, the ID that we appended the link within the block display.

We could have simply chosen to have each title displayed as a link to its node instead of outputting it as a link to `limited-visibility/id`, but then clicking a title would bring up the node page for that node instead of using the display we created. In this example, it wouldn't make much of a difference, but it would if we choose to format the display in a certain way or change the output in some other way to make it different from the node page.

5
Intermediate Custom Theming Views

In this chapter, we will cover:

- ▶ Changing the page template
- ▶ Creating and naming a view template
- ▶ Theming a field
- ▶ Theming a grid
- ▶ Theming a table
- ▶ Theming a row
- ▶ Theming rows
- ▶ Theming an RSS feed
- ▶ Theming a block
- ▶ Theming a view page
- ▶ Theming multiple displays
- ▶ Image styles

Introduction

For anything one needs accomplished in Drupal, there is usually more than one way to do so, and asking a room full of Drupalers to identify the best way will result in many opinions. This is also true with templates.

One can accomplish things in the overall template processing file, `template.php`, in more specific template files, or even in pre-processing files. In some cases, formatting can be accomplished through CSS, whether inline or as part of a CSS file. In this chapter, we will learn to use templates to better format our views.

> If you are using a theme that will be receiving updates from a theme developer or Drupal, you will want to create a sub-theme rather than modify the files of the theme itself; otherwise, your changes will likely be overwritten during any future update. See the article **Sub-theme** structure and inheritance at `http://drupal.org/node/225125`.
>
> The code examples in this chapter use images available for download at `http://packtpub.com` or at `http://theaccidentalcoder.com/content/d7-views-recipes/resources`.

Changing the page template

Templates are available for various formatting needs such as nodes and views. However, the template at the top of the heap, is the page template. In this recipe, we will change the page template in a small way to illustrate how it is done, by moving the footer to the top of the page.

Getting ready

The template file we will be changing is the `page.tpl.php` in the **recipes** theme, a sub-theme in `sites/all/themes/recipes`.

How to do it...

In a text editor of your choice, do the following:

1. Edit the page template file `page.tpl.php` (`sites/all/themes/recipes/templates`).

2. Around line 59, find the following line of code:

   ```php
   <?php print render($page['footer']); ?>
   ```

> **Downloading the example code**
>
> You can download the example code files for all Packt books you have purchased from your account at `http://www.packtpub.com`. If you purchased this book elsewhere, you can visit `http://www.packtpub.com/support` and register to have the files e-mailed directly to you.

We are going to cut this line and paste it just before the following code at about line 56:

```
<?php print render($page['content']); ?>
```

3. Save the file and navigate to the front page to find the **Powered by Drupal** line from the footer, which is now at the top of the content section. If this is the first time you are using this theme, you will need to clear the caches (`admin/settings/performance`), enable the theme, and make it the default theme (`admin/appearance`).

How it works...

A template is simply a file that results in HTML, but uses variables to allow dynamic elements on the page. The page template in Drupal has sections for the regions that are defined in the theme, such as the header, content area, footer, and sidebars. We simply moved the section for the footer from below the main content area to above it.

Creating and naming a view template

The view template is used to make changes to the overall layout of a view, as opposed to a display, table, grid, row, or field within the view. We are going to create a view template from the default template, give a view a title and subtitle, and change the color of its background.

Getting ready

The view that we will be using is **course_list** from *Chapter 3, Intermediate Custom Views*.

How to do it...

Carry out the following steps in order to complete this recipe:

1. Edit the **course_list** view (`admin/structure/views/edit/course_list`).

2. Click on the **Information** link next to **Theme:** in the **Other** pane.

3. In the **Theming information** overlay, ensure that the theme you are using is selected in the select box and then copy the most specific (right-most) filename from the **Display** output line, which, in our case, is `views-view--course-list--page-1.tpl.php`.

4. Copy the `views-view.tpl.php` file from the theme directory of the Views module (`sites/all/modules/views/theme`) to the directory in your theme that contains template files, such as `page.tpl.php` (`sites/all/themes/recipes`), and rename it as `views-view--course-list--page-1.tpl.php`.

Note that in places the filename has one hyphen and in other places two. There is a purpose to this and care must be taken to have the correct amount, when typing the name yourself.

5. Edit the new file, `views-view--course-list--page-1.tpl.php`. Around line 56, look for the following code-line:

```php
<?php if ($rows): ?>
```

Immediately prior to that line, add the following:

```php
<h2>Courses from the D7 Views Recipes University</h2>
<h3>As of <?php echo format_date(time(),

    'custom', 'd F,Y');?></h3>
```

So that the lines, after the copy-paste, read as follows:

```php
<h2>Courses from the D7 Views Recipes University</h2>
<h3>as of <?php echo format_date(time(),
    'custom', 'd F,Y'));?></h3>
<?php if ($rows): ?>
```

6. Save the file and clear the caches. As this is a new template file (`admin/config/development/performance`), navigate to the view (`courses`) to see the resulting headings:

Available Courses

Courses from the D7 Views Recipes University
as of 29 September,2010

Course number	Course	Credits
SP101	Spanish 101	3
EN101	English Composition	3
EN102	English Literature	3
NU301	Introduction to Nursing	4

How it works...

We selected the most specific file available for a template. Take a look at the other filenames in the **Display outline** list. If we had to choose one, we would be dropping the view name, which would then have the file applied to all views. Dropping the display would have it applied to all current and future displays within our view, or both, which would then impact all the displays of all views.

Having selected the appropriate file, by copying the template model from the files available and renaming it, we made the changes to it and applied them. We inserted two titles, and in one, we used a snippet of PHP code to display a formatted date.

There's more...

Inserting HTML and PHP directly into the template file is not always the best approach, but it is the best one that we can use here, as we are creating recipes that can be quickly executed. If 'theming' is new to you, one topic to investigate is that of using the `template.php` file to create variables that can be referred to from within templates, rather than creating them inside a template or using long strings of inline code. It is "the Drupal way" and is a good coding practice to try and keep business logic and presentation logic separated. This means it is very difficult to debug a page where the code can appear anywhere, including within the template that describes the appearance of the page.

Theming a field

Sometimes we want a view to present data from more than one type of content, but doing so doesn't mean that all content types should be presented equally. We could want additional information in some cases, less in others, or, as is the case in this recipe, the same data processed differently.

We are going to create a simple view that displays teasers from all published nodes and create a theme that allows us to create and display the node title links in varying ways, based on the content type.

Getting ready

This view will need at least one node of the content types Article, Country, Course, Employee, and Extension (details are given in *Appendix B, Entity Types and Fields*), and one node from any of the other content types.

How to do it...

Carry out the following steps in order to create the view:

1. Navigate to the **Views** list (`admin/structure/views`), click on the **+Add new view** link, enter **Themed links** as the view title and **Links themed** based on the content type as the view description, and then click on the **Next** button.

2. In the **Display format** section, change the **Teasers** drop-down to **Fields**, **Items per page** to **25**, and click on the **Continue & edit** button.

3. Click on the **+** icon in the **Fields** box, check the box next to **Content: Nid**, **Content: Path**, and **Content: Type**, and then click on the **Add and configure** button.

4. In the configuration box for **Node: Nid**, clear the **Create a label** box and click on the **Apply and continue** button.

5. In the configuration box for **Node: Path**, clear the **Create a label** box and click on the **Apply and continue** button.

6. In the configuration box for **Node: Type**, clear the **Create a label** box and click on the **Apply** button.

7. Click on the **Advanced** link and then the **Information** link next to **Theme:** in the **Other** pane.

8. Scroll down and copy the rightmost filename from the **Row style output** line, `views-view-fields--themed-links--page.tpl.php`.

9. Click on the **Save** button.

Now, create the template:

1. From the **Views** module theme directory (probably `sites/all/modules/views/theme`), copy the file `views-view-fields.tpl.php` and save it into the directory of the theme you are using (`sites/all/themes/your_theme`) that contains template files, naming it **views**-`view-fields--themed-links--page.tpl.php`.

2. Clear your caches (`admin/config/development/performance`).

3. Edit this new file and look around line 22 for the following code line:

```php
<?php foreach ($fields as $id => $field): ?>
```

4. Immediately prior to this line, add the following code:

```php
<?php
  global $base_url;
  $path = $base_url . '/' .
    file_stream_wrapper_get_instance_by_scheme('public')->
      getDirectoryPath() . '/';
  switch ($fields['type']->content) {
  case 'Article':
    $fields['title']->content = "<img src='$path/article.png'
      /> <a href='" . $fields['path']->content . "'>" .
        $fields['title']->content . "</a>";
    break;
  case 'Country':
```

```
    $fields['title']->content = "<img src='$path/country.png'
      /> " . $fields['title']->content;
    break;
  case 'Course':
    $fields['title']->content .= " 
      <a href='http://myschool.edu/courses/?course=" .
        $fields['nid']->content . "'><small>(more info)
          </small></a>";
    break;
  case 'Extension':
    $fields['title']->content = "<a href='" . $fields['path']
      ->content . "'>" . $fields['title']->content .
        "</a> <img src='$path/phone.png' />";
    break;
  case 'Employee':
    $fields['title']->content = "<a href='" . $fields['path']
      ->content . "'><img src='$path/employee.png' border='0'
        /> " . $fields['title']->content . "</a>";
    break;
  default:
    break;
  }
  unset($fields['path']);
  unset($fields['nid']);
  unset($fields['type']);
?>
```

What happened to file_directory_path()?

In Drupal 6, there was a function that returned the path to the files directory relative to the Drupal directory. That function was `file_directory_path()`. In Drupal 7, to obtain the path, use `file_stream_wrapper_get_instance_by_scheme('public')->getDirectoryPath()`.

5. Save the file and navigate to `themed-links` to see the output, as shown in the following screenshot:

 The titles listed and their order could very well vary in your case, as they are being listed in the order in which they were created.

How it works...

The view itself is fairly straightforward. We are selecting all published nodes and are selecting the fields that we will need later for our theme logic, despite the fact that only the title field will be visible.

The reason we did not elect to hide the other fields from being displayed by checking the appropriate box in the field's configuration box is that we want the content of the field available to us in the `$fields` array in the template and it would not be otherwise. We would still have access to it, but in a more convoluted way.

When selecting and creating the file to use for the template, the reason we used the fields-level template instead of field level is that we needed all of the selected fields available at the same time. The fields-level makes each row, node in this case, available as an array of fields, where if we had used the field level, only the individual field would have been visible.

Inside the fields template, each row is processed in a loop, with each field in the row being displayed. We needed to alter the contents of the row before it was printed, so we placed our code before the loop began.

In our code, we changed the value of the title field based on the content type. The switch statement was set up to process the specific content types in which we are interested, but leave the others (`default:`) untouched.

The following is a summary of the content types and what we did with each title:

Article	A document icon, followed by the title linking to the node
Country	A globe icon, followed by the node title
Course	The node title, followed by a (more info) link, including the nid, to an external site
Employee	Both an employee icon and the title as it links to the node
Extension	The title as a link to the node, followed by an icon

Having made the changes to the title field, we no longer had any use for the node ID (`nid`), path, or content type fields, so we unset them, thereby leaving the row loop to find only one field in each row to display, that is, our updated title.

There's more...

Any of the changes we made to the title could have been done individually via the field settings in the views UI, but when needed to account for several different content types and formats, that option is no longer viable.

While you may never have a need to make the same kind of changes that we did here, this method of changing variables within a template can be used to change any selected field or fields.

Theming a grid

One of the presentation types available in a view is the grid. There is a default styling defined for a grid, but you may want the style to be something other than the default. In this recipe, we will alter the formatting of a grid.

Getting ready

We are going to use the same view as the *Theming a field* recipe, but create a new display for it. We will create a table that classifies nodes by content type.

If you have not tried that recipe yet, follow the *Getting ready* section and steps 1-9 of the *How to do it...* section from it, at this point.

How to do it...

On the **View List** page, navigate to the **Views List** (`admin/structure/views`) and click on the **Edit** link for the **themed_links view**.

Carry out the following steps in order to create a new view display:

 Note that in the following steps, references to **Page 1** assume that this is the first page display you have added to the themed_links view. If not, the page number might be different in steps 2, 11, and 13.

1. Click on the **+Add** button in the **Displays** section at the top and select **Page** as the display type.

2. Click on the new **Page 1** link next to **Display name**, enter **Grid Page** as the new name, and then click on the **Apply** button.

3. Click on the **Themed links** link next to **Title**, select **This page (override)**, change the title to **Themed grid**, and click on the **Apply** button.

4. Click **None** next to **Path:** in the **Page settings** pane, enter **themed-grid** as the path, and click on the **Apply** button.

5. Click on the link for **Content: Nid** in the **Fields** box, select **This page (override)** from the select box, and then click on the **Remove** button.

6. Click on the link for **Content: Path** in the **Fields** box, select **This page (override)** from the select box, and then click on the **Remove** button.

7. Click on the **+** icon in the **Fields** box, check the box next to **Content: Body**, and click on the **Add and configure** button.

8. In the configuration box for **Content: Body**, select **This page (override)**, clear the **Create a label** box, select **Summary or trimmed** in the **Formatter** select box, enter **100** for the **Trim length**, and click on the **Apply and continue** button.

9. Click on the **Unformatted list** link next to **Format:** in the **Format** pane, select **This page (override)** from the select box, click on the **Grid** radio button, and then on the **Apply** button.

10. In the **Grid Page: Style** options pane, enter **content-type-[type]** in **Row class**, change the **Number of columns** to **3**, and then click on the **Apply** button.

11. Click on the **Information** link next to **Theme:** in the **Other** pane and copy the rightmost filename from the **Style output** line, that is, `views-view-table--themed-links--page-1.tpl.php`.

12. Click on the **Save** button.

    Now create the template.

13. From the `Views` module theme directory (probably `sites/all/modules/views/theme`), copy the file `views-view-grid.tpl.php` and save it into the directory of the theme you are using (`sites/all/themes/your_theme`) that contains template files, naming it `views-view-grid--themed-links—page-1.tpl.php`.

14. Clear your caches (`admin/config/development/performance`).

15. Edit this new file and look around line 20 for the following:

    ```
    <td class="<?php print $col
      umn_classes[$row_number][$column_number]; ?>">
    ```

16. Immediately prior to this line, add the following:

    ```
    <?php print $row_number * 3 + $column_number; ?>
    ```

17. Save the file.

18. Edit the CSS file for your theme. In my case, it is called `style.css`.

19. Add the following code lines to the file:

    ```
    td.content-type-Article {background-color: #ffc0ff}
    td.content-type-Blog entry {background-color: #c0c0ff}
    td.content-type-Country {background-color: #c0ffc0}
    td.content-type-Course {background-color: #ffffc0}
    td.content-type-Department {background-color: #ffc0c0}
    td.content-type-Destination {background-color: #ffedc1}
    td.content-type-Employee {background-color: #c1ffdb}
    td.content-type-Extension {background-color: #dcc1ff}
    td.content-type-Gallery {background-color: #dcc472}
    td.content-type-Home {background-color: #cadc72}
    td.content-type-Ingredient {background-color: #eebabb}
    td.content-type-Product {background-color: #dff6f7}
    ```

```
td.content-type-Real estate flier {background-color: #f3eeeb}
td.content-type-Sponsor {background-color: #edebf3}
td.content-type-Basic page {background-color: #ffffff}
```

20. Save the file and navigate to `themed-grid` to see the following output:

How it works...

The view selects all published nodes. We created a new page display that shows the title and a teaser from each as a grid cell.

We used a replacement tag [type] as part of the class name for the cell, so that cells can be themed by their content type. In conjunction with this, we added entries to the CSS file to provide a different background color for cells of each content type.

We also created a local copy of the grid template file and edited it to insert a cell number at the top of each cell.

Theming a table

Using the **Style** settings in the Views UI, we can elect to have a view output as table data using an HTML table. Our options, however, as to how the table is structured, are limited. We can overcome these limitations by theming the table output.

Getting ready

We are going to use the same view as the _Theming a field_ recipe, but create a new display for it. We will create a table that classifies nodes by content type.

If you have not tried that recipe yet, go to the _Getting ready_ section and follow steps 1-9 of the _How to do it..._ section from it at this point.

How to do it...

On the **View List** page:

Navigate to the **Views List** (admin/structure/views) and click on the **Edit** link for the **themed_links view**.

1. Create a new view display:

 Note that in the following steps, references to **Page 1** assume that this is the first page display you have added to the **themed_links view**. If not, the page number might be different in steps 2, 10, and 12.

2. Click on the **+Add** button in the **Displays** section at the top and select **Page** as the display type.
3. Click on the new **Page 2** link next to **Name**, enter **Table Page** as the new name, and then click on the **Apply** button.
4. Click on the **Themed links** link next to **Title**, select **This page (override)**, change the title to **Themed table**, and click on the **Apply** button.
5. Click on **None** next to **Path:** in the **Page settings** pane, enter **themed-table** as the path, and click on the **Apply** button.
6. Click on the link for **Content: Post date (desc)** in the **Sort criteria** box, select **This page (override)** from the select box, and then click on the **Remove** button.
7. Click on the link for **Content: Nid** in the **Fields** box, select **This page (override)** from the select box, and then click on the **Remove** button.

8. Click on the link for **Content: Path** in the **Fields** box, select **This page (override)** from the select box, and then click on the **Remove** button.

9. Click on the **Unformatted list** link next to **Format:** in the **Format** pane, select **This page (override)** from the select box, click on the **Table** radio button, and then on the **Apply** button.

10. In the **Table Page: Style options** pane, check both **Sortable** checkboxes and the **Default Sort** radio button for **Content: Title,** and then click on the **Apply** button.

11. Click on the **Information** link next to **Theme:** in the **Other** pane and copy the rightmost filename from the **Style output line**, that is, **views-view-table--themed-links--page-2.tpl.php**.

12. Click on the **Save** button.

Now create the template:

1. From the Views module theme directory (probably `sites/all/modules/views/theme`), copy the file `views-view-table.tpl.php` and save it into the directory of the theme you are using (`sites/all/themes/your_theme`) that contains template files, naming it `views-view-table--themed-links--page-2.tpl.php`.

2. Clear your caches (`admin/config/development/performance`).

3. Edit this new file and look around line 20 for the following line of code:

```
<table class="<?php print $class; ?>">
```

4. Immediately prior to this line, add the following code snippet:

```php
<?php
$header['title'] = 'Title';
$header['Article'] = 'Article';
$header['Country'] = 'Country';
$header['Course'] = 'Course';
$header['Employee'] = 'Employee';
$header['Extension'] = 'Extension';
$header['Other'] = 'Other';
$fields['Article'] = 'type';
$fields['Country'] = 'type';
$fields['Course'] = 'type';
$fields['Employee'] = 'type';
$fields['Extension'] = 'type';
$fields['Other'] = 'type';

foreach ($rows as $count => $row) {
    $rows[$count]['Article'] = ' ';
    $rows[$count]['Country'] = ' ';
    $rows[$count]['Course'] = ' ';
    $rows[$count]['Employee'] = ' ';
    $rows[$count]['Extension'] = ' ';
```

```
        $rows[$count]['Other'] = ' ';
        $type = (in_array($row['type'],array
          ('Article','Country','Course','Employee','Extension'))) ?
            $row['type'] : 'Other';
        $rows[$count][$type] = ($type == 'Other') ?
          $rows[$count]['type'] : 'X';
        unset($rows[$count]['type']);
}
unset($header['type']);
?>
```

5. Save the file, and then navigate to `themed-table` to view something similar to the following screenshot:

Title	Article	Country	Course	Employee	Extension	Other
272					X	
Argentina		X				
Athletics						Department
Australia		X				
Ayen Designs						Sponsor
Beginning Banjo			X			
Biology			X			
Biology Lab			X			
Brazil		X				
Business						Department
Business Management			X			
Canada		X				
China		X				
Chocolate is the New Black of Food						Blog entry
Computer science						Department
DH777777						Home
Early European History			X			
Education						Department
English						Department
English Composition			X			
English Literature			X			
Fine Arts						Department
Fresh Food - More Bang for the Buck!	X					
Functions and Polynomials			X			
Fundamentals of Teaching			X			

1 2 3 next › last »

How it works...

The view selects all published nodes. We created a new page display that formats two fields from each node, the title and content type, as an HTML table. We selected only those two fields because the ultimate table is only meant to display the node title and some manner of showing the content type.

Inside the Table template, there were three portions of the table that we needed to address.

The $header array contains a key for each column that is to have a heading. We added a column to it for each of the several content types, and one catch-all column, titled 'Other', to summarize the content of other types. We also reset the column heading for 'type' that was there due to it being one of the fields we selected within the view. Had we not removed this column heading, the column headings would have been misaligned, making the table data appear to be incorrect.

The $fields array contains an entry for each field that is to be displayed, with the name of the class to be used when displaying it. We added an entry for each of the columns we were adding and ultimately removed the entry $fields['type'], as it would not be needed.

The most important of the three arrays that we manipulated was the $rows array. It contains a key for each column of data to be displayed. We added a column for each of the specific content types that would appear in the table as well as one for 'Other'. We then examined the content type for the row. If the content type matched one of the specific content types (article, country, course, employee, extension), we simply inserted an 'x' into the applicable column for that row. If, however, the content type was other than one of those five, we put the name of the content type into the 'Other' column for that row rather than an 'x' to make it more helpful.

Theming a row

In a record that is selected as a output in a view, there are rows present in the record and often there is a need to format these rows. We will do that with a simple view to make each stand out more than they would otherwise.

Getting ready

We are going to use the Country content type, the details of which are given in *Appendix B, Entity Types and Fields*.

How to do it...

Carry out the following steps in order to create the view:

1. Navigate to the **Views List** (`admin/structure/views`), click on the **+Add new view** link, enter **Country countdown** as the view title, check the **Description** box, and enter **Themed country rows** as the view description.

2. Select **Country** from the **of type** select box.

3. Change **teasers** to **fields** in the **Display format** section and click on the **Continue and edit** button.

4. Click on the **Add** link in the **Fields** pane, check the box next to **Content: Area**, and click on the **Add and configure fields** button.

5. In the configuration box for **Content: Area**, clear the **Create a label** textbox and click on the **Apply and continue** button.

6. Click on the **Add** link in the **Sort Criteria** pane, check the box for **Fields: field_country_area**, and click on the **Apply and configure sort criteria** button.

7. In the configuration overlay, click on the **Apply** button.

8. Click on the link in the **Sort Criteria** pane for **Post date**, select **This page (override)**, and click on the **Remove** button.

9. Click on the **Information** link next to **Theme:** in the **Other** pane and copy the rightmost filename from the **Row style output line**, that is, `views-view-fields--country-countdown--default.tpl.php`.

10. Click on the **Save** button.

Now, create the template:

1. From the Views module `theme` directory (probably `sites/all/modules/views/theme`), copy the file **views-view-fields.tpl.php** and save it into the directory of the theme you are using (`sites/all/themes/your_theme`) that contains template files, naming it as `views-view-fields--country-countdown--default.tpl.php`.

2. Clear your caches (`admin/config/development/performance`).

3. Edit this new file and look around line 22 for the following line of code:

```php
<?php foreach ($fields as $id => $field): ?>
```

4. Immediately prior to this line, add the following code:

```php
<?php global $base_url; ?>
```

5. Then, after the last line in the file, add the following line:

```
<div style="margin: 6px"><img src="<?php echo $base_url . '/' .
    file_stream_wrapper_get_instance_by_scheme('public')->

    getDirectoryPath();?>/country.png" /></div>
```

6. Save the file and navigate to `country-countdown` to see output similar to the following screenshot:

How it works...

The view selects nodes of the Country content type and uses the fields `title` (the country name) and `country_area` (the size of the country). We sorted the countries from the smallest to the largest.

Inside the `Fields` template, we added a graphical divider between each row.

There's more...

There is more that we would like to do with this view, but those changes require us to be able to compare each row to the next row. In this template, we receive one row at a time, and so the template has no knowledge of the rows in bulk. However, the next recipe will address this.

Theming rows

This recipe is attached to the previous one to show the difference between theming a row and theming many rows and because it is important to show how different templates can be used in conjunction with each other.

We are going to make changes to the presentation of the view display and target rows based on their relation to the other rows around them.

Getting ready

If you have not used the previous recipe, _Theming a row_, do so first.

How to do it...

Create the template:

1. From the Views module theme directory (probably `sites/all/modules/views/theme`), copy the file `views-view-unformatted.tpl.php` and save it into the directory of the theme you are using (`sites/all/themes/your_theme`) that contains template files, naming it `views-view-unformatted--country-countdown--page.tpl.php`.

2. Clear your caches (`admin/config/development/performance`).

3. Edit this new file and look around line 10 for the following line of code:

   ```php
   <?php if (!empty($title)): ?>
   ```

4. Immediately prior to this line, add the following code:

   ```css
   <style type="text/css">
   #cc-container {
     width: 180px;
   }
   .cc-odd, .cc-even {
     padding: 6px;
     border: 4px solid black;
     width: 120px;
     position: relative;
     text-align: center;
   ```

```
    }
    .cc-odd {
      left: 0;
      background-color: #aaa;
    }
    .cc-even {
      left: 60px;
      background-color: #eee;
    }
    .cc-value {
      font-size: 36px;
    }
    </style>
    <?php $ctr = sizeof($rows) + 1; ?>
```

5. Find `<?php foreach ($rows as $id => $row) : ?>` at around line 37 and insert the following code line before it:

   ```
   <div id="cc-container">
   ```

6. Find `<div class="<?php print $classes_array[$id]; ?>">` at around line 39 and insert the following lines before it:

   ```
   <div class="cc-<?php echo ($ctr % 2) ? 'odd' : 'even'; ?>">
       <?php $ctr--; ?>
       <div class="cc-value"><?php echo $ctr; ?></div>
   ```

7. Around line 45, find `<?php endforeach; ?>` and add `</div>` on both the line before it and the line after it.

8. The resulting code is as follows:

   ```
   <style type="text/css">
   #cc-container {
     width: 180px;
   }
   .cc-odd, .cc-even {
     padding: 6px;
     border: 4px solid black;
     width: 120px;
     position: relative;
     text-align: center;
   }
   ```

```css
.cc-odd {
  left: 0;
  background-color: #aaa;
}
.cc-even {
  left: 60px;
  background-color: #eee;
}
.cc-value {
  font-size: 36px;
}
</style>
```

```php
<?php $ctr = sizeof($rows) + 1; ?>
<?php if (!empty($title)): ?>
  <h3><?php print $title; ?></h3>
<?php endif; ?>
  <div id="cc-container">
<?php foreach ($rows as $id => $row): ?>
  <div class="cc-<?php echo ($ctr % 2) ? 'odd' : 'even'; ?>">
    <?php $ctr--; ?>
    <div class="cc-value"><?php echo $ctr; ?></div>
      <div class="<?php print $classes_array[$id]; ?>">
        <?php print $row; ?>
      </div>
  </div>
<?php endforeach; ?>
</div>
```

9. Save the file and navigate to `country-countdown` to see output similar to the following screenshot:

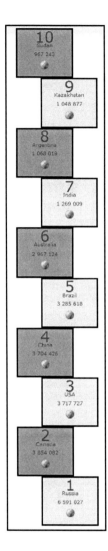

How it works...

We took an existing feed, in which each row is themed, and added a template file to theme at the rows level, also known as the unformatted level. At the row (singular) level, a collection of fields is available for the row currently being processed. At the rows (plural) level, the collection of rows is available.

We added code to the template file that counts down from the number of rows to 1, and styled the output so that the countdown number would display in large text. We also classified each row, based on the counter number, as odd or even by converting the countdown value to binary and calling it even if 0 and odd if 1. We formatted it based on whether the row was odd or even, one being to the right of the other and using a different background color for each.

There's more...

There is so much that can be done at this level. We could, for example, 'pluck' some of the rows, summarize them, and display them in a callout.

We chose to embed a CSS stylesheet within the template file rather than add it to a CSS file. Some would say that all CSS should be in the CSS file, if for no other reason than it is easier for the next person downstream to find it. However, the specification does allow for embedded styles, and if the style is not going to be used anywhere else, keeping it with the code for which it is a unique style also makes sense.

Theming an RSS feed

RSS feeds are used to provide information to other sites about the available content on your site. There are fewer view options for feed displays than for others, because there is an expectation of the format on the receiving end. Still, some formatting can be done, and we will do a little bit of it here while adding a logo to the feed.

Getting ready

We are going to use the Article content type, which is included with Drupal 7.

How to do it...

Carry out the following steps on the **View List** page (`admin/structure/views`):

1. Click on the **+ Add new view** link, enter **Articles** as the view name, check the box for **Description**, and enter **Articles list** as the view description.

2. In the **Type** select box of the **Show line**, select **Article**.

3. Remove the check from the box for **Create a page** and click on the **Continue and Edit** button.

Now create the feed display:

1. Click on the **Add Feed** button to create a new display.

2. Click **None** next to **Path:** in the **Feed settings** panel, enter **articles/feed** as the path, and click on the **Apply** button.

3. Click on the **Information** link next to **Theme:** in the **Other** panel and scroll down and copy the rightmost filename from the Style output line, `views-view- rss-- articles--feed-1.tpl.php`, and click on the **OK** button.

4. Click on the **Save** button.

Now create the template:

1. From the Views module `theme` directory (probably `sites/all/modules/views/ theme`), copy the file `views-view- rss .tpl.php` and save it into the directory of the theme you are using (`sites/all/themes/your_theme`) that contains template files, naming it `views-view -rss--articles--feed-1.tpl.php`.

2. Clear your caches (`admin/config/development/performance`).

3. Edit this new file and look around line 10 for the following code line:

```
<?php print "<?xml"; ?> version="1.0" encoding="utf-8" <?php
   print "?>"; ?>
```

4. Immediately prior to this line, add the following code:

```
<?php global $base_url; ?>
```

5. Then, around line 14, look for :

```
<title><?php print $title; ?></title>
```

6. Insert the following immediately before it:

```
<image>
  <url><?php print $base_url . '/' .
    file_stream_wrapper_get_instance_by_scheme('public')->
      getDirectoryPath() . '/logo.png'; ?></url>
  <title>Ayen Designs logo</title>
  <link><?php print $base_url; ?></link>
</image>
```

7. Save the file and navigate to `articles/feed` to see output similar to the following screenshot:

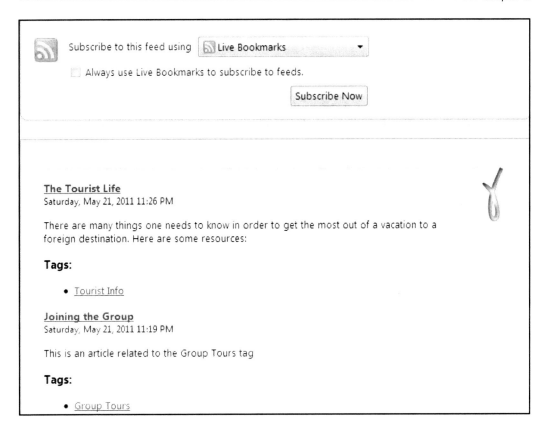

How it works...

We created a simple view that selects the article content and an RSS feed display for it. We then copied the RSS feed template from the Views theme directory, named it so that it would theme our particular view and display, and added XML to the template so our RSS feed page would include a logo.

There's more...

There are a few changes that one can make to RSS feed templates, whether it is the one we worked on or the one that formats the row items, because the RSS specification is XML and only certain elements are defined such as the title and description. The specification does define an image element at the page (channel) level, which is what we used to include an image.

More creative changes can be made to an RSS feed, but to do so requires making changes to the namespace, with which the XML elements are defined. This is outside the scope of this book, but certainly worth investigating if you would like to include, for example, images with your feed elements.

Theming a block

Blocks are ubiquitous in Drupal. With some, the content is inserted manually from the administration panel, in some it is generated within a module, and with others the content comes from a view.

We can theme blocks just like any other display. We will clone an existing block display that lists recent content and make some changes to it via a template, so that it offers a Facebook 'Like' button for each listed content item.

Getting ready

We will be cloning the view from the final recipe (*Creating bulleted lists using multiple content types*) in *Chapter 2, Basic Custom Views*, for this recipe.

How to do it...

Carry out the following steps on the view list page:

1. Navigate to **Views List** (admin/structure/views).
2. Click on the down arrow next to **Edit** for the **Content topics** view and click on the **Clone** link.
3. Enter **Content topics facebook** and click on the **Continue** button.
4. Click on the **edit view name/description** link, enter **Bulleted list of topics with Facebook buttons** as the description, and click on the **Apply** button.
5. Click on the **Table** link next to **Format** in the **Format** pane, click on the radio button for **Unformatted list**, and click on the **Apply** button.
6. Click on the **Apply** button in the subsequent dialog.
7. Click **Grouped contents...** next to **Block name** in the **Block settings** panel, enter **Contents bullet list with Facebook buttons** as the description, and click on the **Apply** button.
8. Click on the link to add a new filter, check the box for **Content: Type**, and click on the **Add and configure filter criteria** button.
9. Check the **Article** checkbox and click on the **Apply** button.
10. Click on the **Content: Type (type)** link in the **Fields** panel and click on the **Remove** button.

11. Click on the link to add a new field, check the boxes for **Content: body** and **Content: Path**, and click on the **Add and configure fields** button.

12. In the **Content: Body** configuration box, clear the **Create a label** textbox, select the **Trimmed in the Formatter** select box, set the **trim length** to **100**, and click on the **Apply default** button.

13. Click on the **Save** button.

14. Click on the **Block** tab and then on the **Information** link next to **Theme:** in the **Other** box and scroll down and copy the rightmost filename from the **Row style output line**, that is, `views-view-fields--content-topics-facebook----block-1.tpl.php`.

Now create the template:

1. From the Views module theme directory (probably `sites/all/modules/views/theme`), copy the file **views-view- fields.tpl.php** and save it into the directory of the theme you are using (`sites/all/themes/your_theme`) that contains template files, naming it as `views-view-fields--content-topics-facebook---block-1.tpl.php`.

2. Clear your caches (`admin/config/development/performance`).

3. Edit this new file and look around line 20 for the following code line:

```
<?php foreach ($fields as $id => $field): ?>
```

4. Prior to this line, insert the following code:

```
<?php
$path = $fields['path']->content;
unset($fields['path']);
?>
```

5. Insert the following code as the final line in the file:

```
<iframe src="<?php print $path; ?>" scrolling="no"
    frameborder="0" allowTransparency="true" style="border:none;
      overflow:hidden; width:120px; height:px"></iframe>
```

6. Save the file.

7. Navigate to the **Blocks Admin** page (`admin/content/block`).

8. Scroll down to the **Disabled** section and set the **Contents bullet list with Facebook** buttons to **Sidebar first** and click on the **Save blocks** button.

9. Navigate to **Home** to view the block, as shown in the following screenshot:

How it works...

We cloned an existing view that produces a bullet list of content titles. We added a field to the selection to capture the node path and specified that only **Articles** were to be selected.

We copied the fields-level template from the `Views theme` folder to our `theme` folder and renamed it so that it would override the formatting of the block from our new view. Inside our template, we set a variable equal to the contents of the node path field and then removed that field from the `$fields` collection so that it would not be printed in the block. We pasted a line of code that creates an IFrame that is loaded from Facebook in the form of a 'Like' button, and within that code snippet, we printed the contents of the field containing the node path, so that each button refers to the proper node.

 Note that the appearance of the IFrame is controlled by Facebook, so it can look different from the preceding screenshot and will look different to logged-in users than those not logged into Facebook.

Theming a view page

Sometimes we will want to make changes to the entire view page display layout to give the page a unique look. The highest level of view template allows us to do that. We will create a view that displays items using a uniquely themed structure.

Getting ready

We are going to use the article list view from the *Theming a RSS feed* recipe.

How to do it...

Carry out the following steps on the **View List** page:

1. Navigate to the **View List** page (`admin/structure/views`).
2. Click on the **Edit** link for the articles list view.

Now create the page display:

1. Click on the **Add** page button.
2. Click on the **Fields** link next to **Show:** in the **Format** pane, click on the radio button for **Content**, and then the **Apply** button.
3. Select **This page (override)** and **Teasers** in the subsequent configuration box and then on the **Apply** button.
4. Click on the **Paged, 10 items** next to **Items to display** in the **Pager** pane, change the **10** to **3** in the **Items per page** textbox, put **1** in the **Number of pages** box, and click on the **Apply** button.
5. Click **None** next to **Path:** in the **Feed settings** box, enter **articles-list** as the path, and click on the **Apply** button.
6. Click on the **Information** link next to **Theme:** in the **Style settings** box and scroll down and copy the rightmost filename from the Style output line, that is, `views-view-unformatted--articles--page-1.tpl.php`.
7. Click on the **Save** button.

Now create the template:

1. From the Views module theme directory (probably `sites/all/modules/views/theme`), copy the file `views-view-unformatted.tpl.php` and save it into the directory of the theme you are using (`sites/all/themes/your_theme`) that contains template files, naming it `views-view-unformatted--articles--page-1.tpl.php`.

2. Clear your caches (`admin/config/development/performance`).

3. Edit this new file and look around line 10 for the following line of code:

```php
<?php if (!empty($title)): ?>
```

4. Insert the following code before it:

```css
<style type="text/css">
.article-1 {
    background-color: #ffaaaa;
    font-size: 14pt;
    border: 4px solid black;
}
.article-2 {
    background-color: #aaffaa;
    font-size: 12pt;
    border: 4px solid black;
}
.article-3 {
    background-color: #aaaaff;
    font-size: 10pt;
    border: 4px solid black;
}
</style>
```

5. Around line 30, find the following code:

```php
<?php //foreach ($rows as $id => $row): ?>
  <div class="<?php //print $classes_array[$id]; ?>">
    <?php //print $row; ?>
  </div>
<?php //endforeach; ?>
```

6. Replace those lines with the following code:

```php
<table id="articles-table">
  <tr>
    <td rowspan="2" class="article-1"><?php print
      $rows[0];?></td>
    <td class="article-2"><?php print $rows[1];?></td>
  </tr>
  <tr>
    <td class="article-3"><?php print $rows[2];?></td>
  </tr>
</table>
```

7. Save the file and navigate to `articles-list` to see a screen similar to the following screenshot:

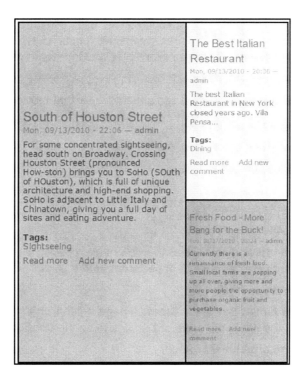

How it works...

We created a page display that selects three article nodes. We did not bother with verifying the selection within the template for this exercise, being comfortably assured that there will be at least three articles in our project site to draw from. We then modified the view template that receives the selection rows as a collection and instead of looping through them and printing each one the same as the last, we printed each individually with specific formatting in mind.

We used a stylesheet internal to the template rather than the CSS file. We also used a table to format the three records rather than just CSS and `<div>`; the reason being that forcing the left column (record 1 of 3) to be of the same height as the two stacked to its right using only CSS requires CSS hacks beyond the scope of this book.

There's more...

This recipe showed how to manipulate a collection of rows within one display, but we can do even more than that. We can have multiple displays in one view, all being displayed simultaneously, and manipulate the data for them. We will do that in the next recipe.

Theming multiple displays

Having multiple displays displayed simultaneously allows us to use parts of the viewing area for distinct but related displays and, if desired, interactive functionality, much like a desktop application. This enables an enhanced user experience and increased value from your site.

In this recipe, we will have a display that lists available courses, another that lists departments, which drives the course list, and a third display that provides course details. This view will also make use of contextual filters. Information about the Course and Department content types can be found in *Appendix B, Entity Types and Field*s.

How to do it...

Carry out the following steps on the **View List** page (`admin/structure/views`):

1. Click on the **+ Add new view** link.

2. Enter **Departments and courses** as the view name, check the box for **Description**, and enter **Interactive course and department listing** as the view description.

3. Change **Sorted by** to **Title**.

4. On the **Display format line** of the **Create a page** section, change **Teasers** to **full posts**, change the **Items per page** to **1**, and click on the **Continue and edit** button.

5. Click on the **Add attachment** button.

6. Click on the **Attachment 2** link next to **Display name:**, change the name to **Department list**, and click on the **Apply** button.

7. Click on the **Add attachment** button.

8. Click on the **Attachment** link next to **Display name:**, change the name to **Course list**, and click on the **Apply** button.

Create the Course list attachment:

1. Click on the tab for **Course list1**.

2. Click on the **Content** link next to **Show:** in the **Format** section, change **All displays** to **This attachment (override)**, click on the **Fields** radio button, and click on the **Apply** button.

3. Click on the **Apply** button on the subsequent **Row style options** screen.

4. Click on the link in the **Fields** pane to add a field, check the box for **Content: Nid**, and click on the button for **Add and configure fields**.

5. Select **This attachment (override)**, check the box for **Exclude from display**, and click on the **Apply** button.

6. In the **Fields** select box, select **Rearrange**, drag the **Nid** field before the **Title field**, and click on the **Apply** button.

7. Click on the **Content: Title** link in the **Fields** pane, select **This attachment (override)**, and remove the check from the **Link this field to the original piece of content** checkbox

8. Click on the **Rewrite Results** link to reveal its settings and check the **Output this field as a link** checkbox.

9. In the **Link path** textbox, enter **departments-and-courses/!1/[nid]** and click on the **Apply** button.

10. Click on the link in the **Filter** pane to add a new filter.

11. Check the box for **Content: Type** and click on the button for **Add and configure filter criteria**, select **This attachment (override)**, check the box for **Course**, and click on the **Apply** button.

12. In the **Attachment settings** panel, click on the **Not defined** link next to **Attach to**, check the box for **Page**, and click on the **Apply** button.

 Always check to see which tab is highlighted before making an edit. Sometimes saving an edit returns you to the first display.

13. Click on the link for **Before next to Position:**, change the setting to **After**, and click on the **Apply** button.

Now create the Department list attachment:

1. Click on the tab for **Department list**2.

2. Click on the **Content** link next to **Show:** in the **Format** section, change **All displays** to **This attachment (override)**, click on the **Fields** radio button, and click on the **Apply** button.

3. Click on the **Apply** button on the subsequent **Row style options** screen.

4. If the **Fields** pane does not already contain **Content: Nid**, click on the link in the **Fields** pane to add a field, check the box for **Content: Nid**, and click on the button for the **Add and configure fields**.

5. Select **This attachment (override)**, check the box for **Exclude from display**, and click on the **Apply** button.

6. In the **Fields** select box select **Rearrange**, drag the **Nid** field before the **Title** field and click on the **Apply** button.

7. Click on the **Content: Title** link in the **Fields** pane, select **This attachment (override)**, and remove the check from **Link this field to the original piece of content**. Click on the **Rewrite Results** link to reveal its settings and check the **Output this field as a link** checkbox.

8. In the **Link path** text box, enter **departments-and-courses/[nid]** and click on the **Apply** button.

9. In the **Attachment settings** panel, click on the **Not defined** link next to **Attach to**, check the box for **Page**, and click on the **Apply** button.

10. Ensure that the position for the attachment is listed as **Before** rather than **After**.

11. Click on the link to add a relationship, check the box for **Fields: Department (field_department_ref) – nid**, and click on the **Add and configure relationships** button.

12. Select **This attachment (override)** and click on the **Apply** button.

Now complete the page display:

1. Click on the **Page** tab.

2. Click on the link to add a new filter, check the box for **Content: Type**, and click on the **Add and configure filter criteria** button.

3. Select **This page (override)**, check the **Course** checkbox, and then click on the **Apply** button.

4. Click on the **Paged, 10 items** next to **Items to display** in the **Pager** pane, change the **10** to **1** in the **Items per page** text box, put **1** in the **Number of pages** textbox, and click on the **Apply** button.

5. Click **None** next to **Path:** in the **Feed settings** box, enter **departments-and-courses** as the path, and click on the **Apply** button.

6. Click on the **Advanced** link, if the **Advanced** pane is not visible.

7. Click on the **+ Add** link in the **Contextual filters** pane, check the box for **Global: Null**, and click on the **Apply and configure contextual filters** button.

8. Select **This page (override)**. Beneath **When the filter value is NOT in the URL**, click on the radio button for **Display contents of "No results found"** and click on the **Apply** button.

9. Click on the **+ Add** link in the **Contextual filters** pane, check the box for **Content: Nid**, and click on the **Apply and configure contextual filters** button.

10. Select **This page (override)**. Beneath **When the filter value is NOT in the URL**, click on the radio button for **Display contents of "No results found"** and click on the **Apply** button.

11. Click on the **+ Add** link for **No results behavior**, select **Global: Text area**, and click on the **Add** button.

12. In the subsequent configuration pane, select **This page (override)**, enter **Select a course** as the Label, enter **<h2>Please select a department and then a course</h2>** in the textbox, select **Full HTML** from the **Text format** select box, and click on the **Apply** button.

13. Click on the **Information** link next to **Theme:** in the **Style settings** box. Scroll down and copy the rightmost filename from the Display output line, that is, **views-view--departments-and-courses--page.tpl.php**.

14. Click on the **Save** button.

Now, create the template:

1. From the Views module theme directory (probably `sites/all/modules/views/theme`), copy the file **views-view-unformatted.tpl.php** and save it into the directory of the theme you are using (`sites/all/themes/your_theme`) that contains the template files, naming it `views-view-unformatted--articles--page-1.tpl.php`.

2. Clear your caches (`admin/config/development/performance`).

3. Edit this new file and look around line 52 for the following code:

```php
<?php if ($attachment_before): ?>
  <div class="attachment attachment-before">
    <?php print $attachment_before; ?>
  </div>
<?php endif; ?>
```

4. Cut it and paste it around line 66, just before the following line of code:

```php
<?php if ($attachment_after): ?>
```

5. On line 77, enter the following line of code:

```html
<div style="clear:both"></div>
```

6. Edit your theme's CSS file (in my case, it is `style.css`) and add the following at the bottom of the file:

```css
page-departments-and-courses .attachment-before,
.page-departments-and-courses .attachment-after {
border: 2px solid black;
width: 46%;
min-height: 300px;
background-color: #eee;
float: left;
padding: 3px;
}
```

7. Save the file, clear your caches, and navigate to `departments-and-courses`, which should look similar to the following screenshot:

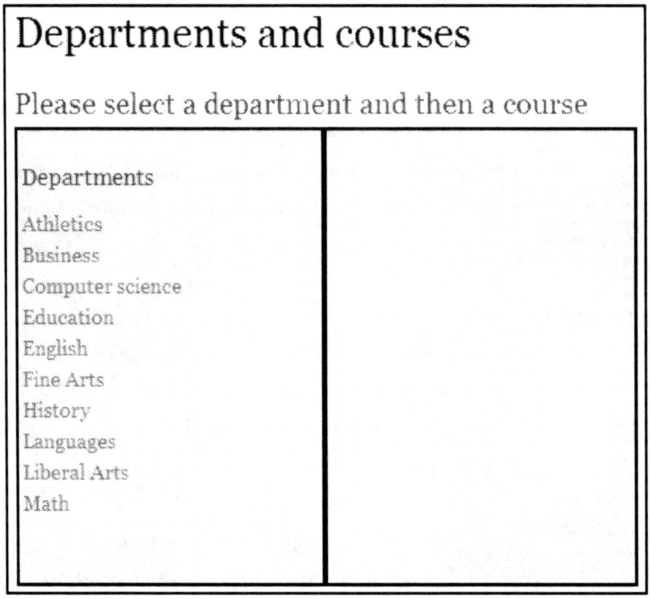

Departments and courses

Please select a department and then a course

Departments	
Athletics	
Business	
Computer science	
Education	
English	
Fine Arts	
History	
Languages	
Liberal Arts	
Math	

8. Click on a department name:

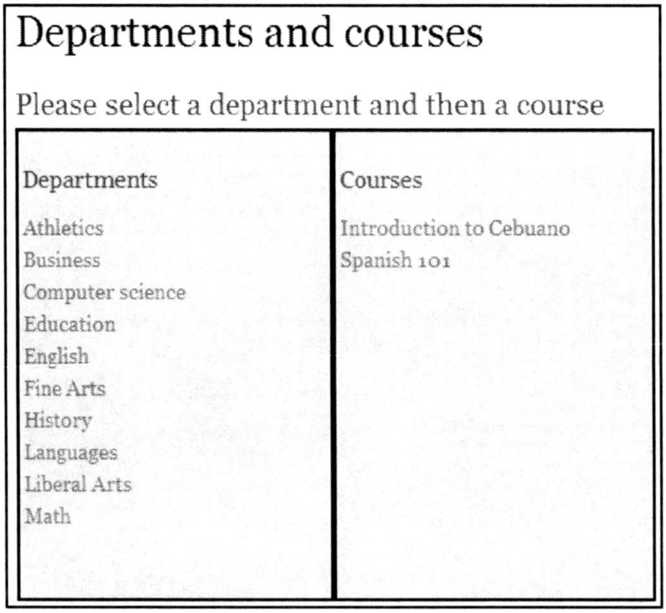

Departments and courses

Please select a department and then a course

Departments	Courses
Athletics	Introduction to Cebuano
Business	Spanish 101
Computer science	
Education	
English	
Fine Arts	
History	
Languages	
Liberal Arts	
Math	

9. Click on any course for that department:

Departments and courses

Introduction to Cebuano
Submitted by ayen on Mon, 07/04/2011 - 19:33

The Visayas are the jewel of the Philippines, and the crown jewel o
the Visayas is Cebu. Introduction to Cebuano focuses on
pronunciation, common greetings and expressions, sentence
structure and present tense verbs.

Prerequisite: Spanish 101

Course number:
CEB102
Course credits:
3
Department:
Languages

Departments	Courses
Athletics	Introduction to Cebuano
Business	Spanish 101
Computer science	
Education	
English	
Fine Arts	
History	
Languages	
Liberal Arts	
Math	

How it works...

The secret to this recipe is the use of Attachment displays to augment the normal content of the Page display and moving data between the steps.

The first step is to display a list of departments in the first Attachment display, and to rewrite the department titles as links back to the same page, departments-and-courses, but containing an argument, which is the department node ID (nid) such as departments-and-courses/32.

The second attachment display is to display a list of courses, but only those courses that belong to the received department number. We again rewrite the output as links of the title, in this case, the course title, but this time, we pass an additional argument, the `nid` of the course.

The page display provides the course details and uses the second passed argument to identify which course to display.

We also configured the view to display a message when the view is requested without any argument.

We edited the view template to move the previous attachment to appear after the content, and then edited the CSS file to format the two attachments and have them appear side-by-side.

There's more...

For more information on using multiple displays, *"Drupal 6 Attachment Views"*, *Packt Publishing* at `https://www.packtpub.com/drupal-6-attachment-views/book`.

Image styles

There are many different venues in a website for images to be displayed from the same source, but with a different appearance for each image. In Drupal 6, this was achieved via a contributed module, **ImageCache**. That module has since been incorporated into Drupal itself, and we will use that functionality to display images in three different sizes.

Getting ready

1. We are going to use the Gallery content type. If you have not already added it, you will find the details in *Appendix B, Entity Types and Fields*.

2. You will need four pieces of gallery content.

3. There will be three image styles used, namely, `Exhibit`, `Exhibit_teaser`, and `Exhibit_block`, the details of which are in *Appendix B, Entity Types and Fields*.

How to do it...

1. Navigate to the views list (`admin/structure/views`).

2. Click on the **+ Add new view** link, enter **Image styles** as the view name, check the **Description** box, enter **Use image styles with view displays** as the view description, and change **All** to **Gallery** in **Show content of type**.

3. In the **Create a page** section, change **Teasers** to **Fields** for the **Display format** and change **Items per page** to **1**.

4. Check the box to **Create a block**, change **Titles (linked)** to **Fields** for **Display format**, change the **Items to display** to **1**, and click on the **Continue & edit button**.

Now edit the page display:

1. Click on the **add** link in the **Filters Criteria** box, check the box next to **Fields: Exhibit image (field_exhibit_image) - fid**, and click on the **Add and configure filter criteria** button.

2. In the configuration box for **Fields: Exhibit image (field_exhibit_image) - fid**, select **Is not empty (NOT NULL)** from the select box and click the **Apply** button.

3. Click on the **add** link next to **Fields**, check the box next to **Content: Body**, next to **Content: Exhibit image**, and click on the **Add and configure fields** button.

4. In the **Fields: body** configuration box, change **All displays** to **This page (override)**, clear the **Create a label** checkbox, and click the **Apply** button.

5. In the **Content: Exhibit image** configuration box, clear the **Create a label** textbox, select **exhibit** from the **Image style** select box, and click on the **Apply** button.

6. Click on the **Full** link next to **Use pager:** in the **Pager** pane, select **This page (override)**, change the selection to **Display a specified number of items**, and click on the **Apply** button.

Now edit the block display:

1. Click on the **Block** tab in the **Displays** list at the top of the page.

2. Click on the **add** link next to **Fields**, check the box next to **Content: Exhibit image**, and click on the **Add and configure fields** button.

3. In the **Content: Exhibit image** configuration box, select **This block (override)** from the select box, clear the **Create a label** checkbox, select **exhibit_block** from the **Image style** select box, select **Content** from the **Link image to** select box, and click on the **Apply** button.

4. Click on the **Full** link next to **Use pager:** in the **Pager** pane, select **This block (override),** change the selection to **Display a specified number of items,** and click on the **Apply** button, as shown in the following screenshot:

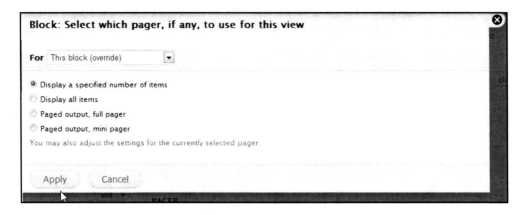

5. Click on the **1 item** link next to **Use pager:** in the **Pager** pane, change **0** to **1** in the **Offset** field, change **0** to **1** in the **Pager ID** field, and click on the **Apply** button.

Now create the attachment display:

1. Click the **+ Add display** button and click on the **Attachment** link.

2. In the **Attachment settings** pane, click **Before** next to **Attachment position,** click on the radio button for **After,** and click on the **Apply** button.

3. Also in the **Attachment settings** pane, click **Not defined** next to **Attach to,** click on the checkbox for **Page,** and click on the **Apply** button.

4. Click the **Content: Exhibit** image link in the **Fields** pane, select **This attachment (override)** from the select box, clear the **Create a label** textbox, select **exhibit_teaser** from the **Image style** select box, and click on the **Apply** button.

5. Click on the **Full** link next to **Use pager:** in the **Pager** pane, select **This attachment (override),** change the selection to **Display a specified number of items,** and click on the **Apply** button.

6. Click on **10 items** next to **Items to display:** in the **Pager** pane, change **Items to display** to **2** and **Offset** to **2,** and then click on the **Apply** button.

7. Click the on **Save** button.

8. Navigate to admin/structure/block, find **image_styles: Block** in the **Disabled** list, select a sidebar from the **Region** select box, click on the **Save blocks** button, scroll up to the same entry, which is now in the section for the sidebar that you selected, and click on its **Configure** link.

9. Under **Show block on specific pages**, select **Only the listed pages** and enter **image-styles** in the text area box, and then click on the **Save block** button.

10. Navigate to `image-styles` to see the view, as shown in the following screenshot:

How it works...

When an image style is created, that style is made available for any image field, including wherever that image field is used in a view. We created three image styles of different sizes and used each style in a different display in the same view.

One other thing we did was to set offsets in the paging pane for each display. The page display chose the most recent image. The block had an offset of 1, so it chose the second most recent image, and the attachment display with its offset of 2 ended up choosing the third and fourth most recent images.

With the image style feature, there is no need to upload multiple images simply to have different sizes. Just make sure to upload the largest size that you will use, because scaling it down in size is fine.

6
Creating Views Programmatically

In this chapter, we will cover:

- ▶ Programming a view
- ▶ Handling a view feld
- ▶ Styling a view feld
- ▶ Fine tuning the query

Introduction

In this chapter, we will switch from the admin user interface to code, creating a view within a module and other examples of using code in conjunction with Drupal and Views architectures to manipulate the content. These methods should only be considered if you are comfortable with PHP and the Drupal architecture and API. The benefits of using code include more granular control, as well as the ability to achieve behaviors otherwise unavailable. The drawbacks are that the Views environment can be very complex, and one can easily break the environment.

The differences between using the Views UI to create a view and doing it in a module is that the UI does the coding for you and makes it more convenient to make changes to the view afterwards. That said, the UI method does *not* make it easy to distribute a ready-made view, nor does it make it facilitate tying such a view to other code.

Programming a view

Creating a view with a module is a convenient way to have a predefined view available with Drupal. As long as the module is installed and enabled, the view will be there to be used. If you have never created a module in Drupal, or even never written a line of Drupal code, you will still be able to create a simple view using this recipe.

Getting ready

Creating a module involves the creation of the following two files at a minimum:

▶ An `.info` file that gives Drupal the information needed to add the module

▶ A `.module` file that contains the PHP script

More complex modules will consist of more files, but those two are all we will need for now.

How to do it...

Carry out the following steps:

1. Create a new directory named `_custom` inside your contributed modules directory (so, probably `sites/all/modules/_custom`).

2. Create a subdirectory inside that directory; we will name it `d7vr` (Drupal 7 Views Recipes).

3. Open a new file with your editor and add the following lines:

```
; $Id:
name = Programmatic Views
description = Provides supplementary resources such as
  programmatic views
package = D7 Views Recipes

version = "7.x-1.0"
core = "7.x"
php = 5.2
```

4. Save the file as `d7vrpv.info`.

5. Open a new file with your editor and add the following lines:

> Feel free to download this code from the author's web site rather than typing it at `http://theaccidentalcoder.com/content/drupal-7-views-cookbook`.

```php
<?php
/**
 * Implements hook_views_api().
 */
function d7vrpv_views_api() {
  return array(
    'api' => 2,
    'path' => drupal_get_path('module', 'd7vrpv'),
  );
}
/**
 * Implements hook_views_default_views().
 */
function d7vrpv_views_default_views() {
  return d7vrpv_list_all_nodes();
}
/**
 * Begin view
 */
function d7vrpv_list_all_nodes() {
  /*
   * View 'list_all_nodes'
   */
  $view =   views_new_view();
  $view->name = 'list_all_nodes';
  $view->description = 'Provide a list of node titles,
    creation dates, owner and status';
  $view->tag = '';
  $view->view_php = '';
  $view->base_table = 'node';
  $view->is_cacheable = FALSE;
  $view->api_version = '3.0-alpha1';
  $view->disabled = FALSE; /* Edit this to true to make a
    default view disabled initially */

/* Display: Defaults */
  $handler = $view->new_display('default', 'Defaults', 'default');
  $handler->display->display_options['title'] = 'List All Nodes';
  $handler->display->display_options['access']['type'] = 'role';
  $handler->display->display_options['access']['role'] = array(
    '3' => '3',
  );
  $handler->display->display_options['cache']['type'] = 'none';
```

```
$handler->display->display_options['exposed_form']['type'] =
  'basic';
$handler->display->display_options['pager']['type'] = 'full';
$handler->display->
  display_options['pager']['options']['items_per_page'] = '15';
$handler->display->display_options['pager']['options']
  ['offset'] = '0';
$handler->display->display_options['pager']['options']
  ['id'] = '0';
$handler->display->display_options['style_plugin'] = 'table';
$handler->display->display_options['style_options']
  ['columns'] = array(
  'title' => 'title',
  'type' => 'type',
  'created' => 'created',
  'name' => 'name',
  'status' => 'status',
);
$handler->display->display_options['style_options']
  ['default'] = 'created';
$handler->display->display_options['style_options']
  ['info'] = array(
  'title' => array(
    'sortable' => 1,
    'align' => 'views-align-left',
    'separator' => '',
  ),
  'type' => array(
    'sortable' => 1,
    'align' => 'views-align-left',
    'separator' => '',
  ),
  'created' => array(
    'sortable' => 1,
    'align' => 'views-align-left',
    'separator' => '',
  ),
  'name' => array(
    'sortable' => 1,
    'align' => 'views-align-left',
    'separator' => '',
  ),
  'status' => array(
    'sortable' => 1,
    'align' => 'views-align-left',
```

```
      'separator' => '',
    ),
  );
$handler->display->display_options['style_options']
  ['override'] = 1;
$handler->display->display_options['style_options']
  ['sticky'] = 0;
$handler->display->display_options['style_options']
  ['order'] = 'desc';
/* Header: Global: Text area */
$handler->display->display_options['header']['area']
  ['id'] = 'area';
$handler->display->display_options['header']['area']
  ['table'] = 'views';
$handler->display->display_options['header']['area']
  ['field'] = 'area';
$handler->display->display_options['header']['area']
  ['empty'] = TRUE;
$handler->display->display_options['header']['area']
  ['content'] = '<h2>Following is a list of all non-page
  nodes.</h2>';
$handler->display->display_options['header']['area']
  ['format'] = '3';
/* Footer: Global: Text area */
$handler->display->display_options['footer']['area']
  ['id'] = 'area';
$handler->display->display_options['footer']['area']
  ['table'] = 'views';
$handler->display->display_options['footer']['area']
  ['field'] = 'area';
$handler->display->display_options['footer']['area']
  ['empty'] = TRUE;
$handler->display->display_options['footer']['area']
  ['content'] = '<small>This view is brought to you courtesy
    of the D7 Views Recipes module</small>';
$handler->display->display_options['footer']['area']
  ['format'] = '3';
/* Field: Node: Title */
$handler->display->display_options['fields']['title']
  ['id'] = 'title';
$handler->display->display_options['fields']['title']
  ['table'] = 'node';
$handler->display->display_options['fields']['title']
  ['field'] = 'title';
$handler->display->
  display_options['fields']['title']['alter']['alter_text'] = 0;
```

```
$handler->display->
  display_options['fields']['title']['alter']['make_link'] = 0;
$handler->display->
  display_options['fields']['title']['alter']['trim'] = 0;
$handler->display->
  display_options['fields']['title']['alter']
    ['word_boundary'] = 1;
$handler->display->
  display_options['fields']['title']['alter']['ellipsis'] = 1;
$handler->display->
  display_options['fields']['title']['alter']['strip_tags'] = 0;
$handler->display->
  display_options['fields']['title']['alter']['html'] = 0;
$handler->display->
  display_options['fields']['title']['hide_empty'] = 0;
$handler->display->
  display_options['fields']['title']['empty_zero'] = 0;
$handler->display->
  display_options['fields']['title']['link_to_node'] = 0;
/* Field: Node: Type */
$handler->display->display_options['fields']['type']
  ['id'] = 'type';
$handler->display->display_options['fields']['type']
  ['table'] = 'node';
$handler->display->display_options['fields']['type']
  ['field'] = 'type';
$handler->display->
  display_options['fields']['type']['alter']['alter_text'] = 0;
$handler->display->
  display_options['fields']['type']['alter']['make_link'] = 0;
$handler->display->
  display_options['fields']['type']['alter']['trim'] = 0;
$handler->display->
  display_options['fields']['type']['alter']
    ['word_boundary'] = 1;
$handler->display->
  display_options['fields']['type']['alter']['ellipsis'] = 1;
$handler->display->
  display_options['fields']['type']['alter']['strip_tags'] = 0;
$handler->display->
  display_options['fields']['type']['alter']['html'] = 0;
$handler->display->
  display_options['fields']['type']['hide_empty'] = 0;
$handler->display->
  display_options['fields']['type']['empty_zero'] = 0;
$handler->display->
  display_options['fields']['type']['link_to_node'] = 0;
```

```
$handler->display->
  display_options['fields']['type']['machine_name'] = 0;
/* Field: Node: Post date */
$handler->display->display_options['fields']['created']
  ['id'] = 'created';
$handler->display->display_options['fields']['created']
  ['table'] = 'node';
$handler->display->display_options['fields']['created']
  ['field'] = 'created';
$handler->display->
  display_options['fields']['created']['alter']
    ['alter_text'] = 0;
$handler->display->
  display_options['fields']['created']['alter']
    ['make_link'] = 0;
$handler->display->
  display_options['fields']['created']['alter']['trim'] = 0;
$handler->display->
  display_options['fields']['created']['alter']
    ['word_boundary'] = 1;
$handler->display->
  display_options['fields']['created']['alter']['ellipsis'] = 1;
$handler->display->
  display_options['fields']['created']['alter']
    ['strip_tags'] = 0;
$handler->display->
  display_options['fields']['created']['alter']['html'] = 0;
$handler->display->
  display_options['fields']['created']['hide_empty'] = 0;
$handler->display->
  display_options['fields']['created']['empty_zero'] = 0;
$handler->display->
  display_options['fields']['created']['date_format'] =
    'custom';
$handler->display->
  display_options['fields']['created']['custom_date_format'] =
    'Y-m-d';
/* Field: User: Name */
$handler->display->display_options['fields']['name']
  ['id'] = 'name';
$handler->display->display_options['fields']['name']
  ['table'] = 'users';
$handler->display->display_options['fields']['name']
  ['field'] = 'name';
$handler->display->display_options['fields']['name']
  ['label'] = 'Author';
```

```
$handler->display->
  display_options['fields']['name']['alter']['alter_text'] = 0;
$handler->display->
  display_options['fields']['name']['alter']['make_link'] = 0;
$handler->display->
  display_options['fields']['name']['alter']['trim'] = 0;
$handler->display->
  display_options['fields']['name']['alter']
    ['word_boundary'] = 1;
$handler->display->
  display_options['fields']['name']['alter']['ellipsis'] = 1;
$handler->display->
  display_options['fields']['name']['alter']['strip_tags'] = 0;
$handler->display->
  display_options['fields']['name']['alter']['html'] = 0;
$handler->display->
  display_options['fields']['name']['hide_empty'] = 0;
$handler->display->
  display_options['fields']['name']['empty_zero'] = 0;
$handler->display->
  display_options['fields']['name']['link_to_user'] = 0;
$handler->display->
  display_options['fields']['name']['overwrite_anonymous'] = 0;
/* Field: Node: Published */
$handler->display->display_options['fields']['status']
  ['id'] = 'status';
$handler->display->display_options['fields']['status']
  ['table'] = 'node';
$handler->display->display_options['fields']['status']
  ['field'] = 'status';
$handler->display->
  display_options['fields']['status']['alter']
  ['alter_text'] = 0;
$handler->display->
  display_options['fields']['status']['alter']['make_link'] = 0;
$handler->display->
  display_options['fields']['status']['alter']['trim'] = 0;
$handler->display->
  display_options['fields']['status']['alter']
    ['word_boundary'] = 1;
$handler->display->
  display_options['fields']['status']['alter']['ellipsis'] = 1;
$handler->display->
  display_options['fields']['status']['alter']
    ['strip_tags'] = 0;
$handler->display->
  display_options['fields']['status']['alter']['html'] = 0;
```

```
$handler->display->
  display_options['fields']['status']['hide_empty'] = 0;
$handler->display->
  display_options['fields']['status']['empty_zero'] = 0;
$handler->display->display_options['fields']['status']
  ['type'] = 'true-false';
$handler->display->display_options['fields']['status']
  ['not'] = 0;
/* Sort criterion: Node: Post date */
$handler->display->display_options['sorts']['created']
  ['id'] = 'created';
$handler->display->display_options['sorts']['created']
  ['table'] = 'node';
$handler->display->display_options['sorts']['created']
  ['field'] = 'created';
$handler->display->display_options['sorts']['created']
  ['order'] = 'DESC';
/* Filter: Node: Type */
$handler->display->display_options['filters']['type']
  ['id'] = 'type';
$handler->display->display_options['filters']['type']
  ['table'] = 'node';
$handler->display->display_options['filters']['type']
  ['field'] = 'type';
$handler->display->
  display_options['filters']['type']['operator'] = 'not in';
$handler->display->display_options['filters']['type']
  ['value'] = array(
    'page' => 'page',
  );

/* Display: Page */
$handler = $view->new_display('page', 'Page', 'page_1');
$handler->display->display_options['path'] = 'list-all-nodes';
$views[$view->name] = $view;

return $views;
}
?>
```

6. Save the file as d7vrpv.module.

7. Navigate to the modules admin page at **admin/modules**.

8. Scroll down to the new module and activate it, as shown in the following screenshot:

ENABLED	NAME	VERSION	DESCRIPTION	OPERATIONS
✓	**Programmatic Views**	7.x-1.0	Provides supplementary resources such as programmatic views	

▼ D7 VIEWS RECIPES

9. Navigate to the **Views Admin** page (`admin/structure/views`) to verify that the view appears in the list:

ⓘ *Normal* Node view: **limited_visibility**	Edit | Export | Clone | Delete
Path: limited-visibility	Present the user's content
Block, Page	

10. Finally, navigate to **list-all-nodes** to see the view, as shown in the following screenshot:

Following is a list of all non-page nodes.

Title	Type	Post date ▲	Author	Published
Published Node 1	Article	2010-06-15	admin	True
Unpublished node 1	Article	2010-06-15	admin	False
Unpublished node 2	Article	2010-06-15	admin	False
Test Article 1	Article	2010-07-05	admin	True
Test Article 2	Article	2010-07-05	admin	True
Unpublished article	Article	2010-07-05	admin	False
Heracles	Gallery	2010-07-11	admin	True
Mona Lisa	Gallery	2010-07-11	admin	True
Ayen Designs	Sponsor	2010-07-17	admin	True
TheAccidentalCoder.com	Sponsor	2010-07-17	admin	True
Packt Publishing	Sponsor	2010-07-17	admin	True
Hand-carved Floor Mirror	Product	2010-07-26	admin	True
M999999	Home	2010-07-31	admin	True
WH888888	Home	2010-07-31	admin	True
DH777777	Home	2010-08-01	admin	True

1 2 3 4 5 next › last »

This view is brought to you courtesy of the D7 Views Recipes module

How it works...

The module we have just created could have many other features associated with it, beyond simply a view, and enabling the module will make those features and the view available, while disabling it will hide those same features and view.

When compiling the list of installed modules, Drupal looks first in its own modules directory for `.info` files, and then in the site's modules directories. As can be deduced from the fact that we put our `.info` file in a second-level directory of `sites/all/modules` and it was found there, Drupal will traverse the modules directory tree looking for `.info` files.

We created a `.info` file that provided Drupal with the name and description of our module, its version, the version of Drupal it is meant to work with, and a list of files used by the module, in our case just one.

We saved the `.info` file as `d7vrpv.info` (Drupal 7 Views Recipes programmatic view); the name of the directory in which the module files appear (d7vr) has no bearing on the module itself.

The module file contains the code that will be executed, at least initially. Drupal does not "call" the module code in an active way. Instead, there are **events** that occur during Drupal's creation of a page, and modules can elect to register with Drupal to be notified of such events when they occur, so that the module can provide the code to be executed at that time; for example, you registering with a business to receive an e-mail in the event of a sale. Just like you are free to act or not, but the sales go on regardless, so too Drupal continues whether or not the module decides to do something when given the chance.

Our module 'hooks' the `views_api` and `views_default_views` events in order to establish the fact that we do have a view to offer. The latter hook instructs the Views module which function in our code executes our view: `d7vrpv_list_all_nodes()`. The first thing it does is create a view object by calling a function provided by the Views module. Having instantiated the new object, we then proceed to provide the information it needs, such as the name of the view, its description, and all the information that we would have selected through the Views UI had we used it. As we are specifying the view options in the code, we need to provide the information that is needed by each **handler** of the view functionality.

The net effect of the code is that when we have cleared cache and enabled our module, Drupal then includes it in its list of modules to poll during events. When we navigate to the **Views Admin** page, an event occurs in which any module wishing to include a view in the list on the admin screen does so, including ours. One of the things our module does is define a path for the page display of our view, which is then used to establish a callback. When that path, `list-all-nodes`, is requested, it results in the function in our module being invoked, which in turn provides all the information necessary for our view to be rendered and presented.

There's more...

The details of the code provided to each handler are outside the scope of this book, but you don't really need to understand it all in order to use it.

You can enable the **Views Bulk Export** module (it comes with Views), create a view using the Views UI in admin, and choose to Bulk Export it. Give the exporter the name of your new module and it will create a file and populate it with nearly all the code necessary for you.

Handling a view field

As you may have noticed in the preceding code that you typed or pasted, Views makes tremendous use of handlers. What is a handler? It is simply a script that performs a special task on one or more elements. Think of a house being built. The person who comes in to tape, mud, and sand the wallboard is a handler.

In Views, one type of handler is the **field handler**, which handles any number of things, from providing settings options in the field configuration dialog, to facilitating the field being retrieved from the database if it is not part of the primary record, to rendering the data. We will create a field handler in this recipe that will add to the display of a zip code a string showing how many other nodes have the same zip code, and we will add some formatting options to it in the next recipe.

Getting ready

A handler lives inside a module, so we will create one:

1. Create a directory in your contributed modules path for this module.

2. Open a new text file in your editor and paste the following code into it:

```
; $Id:
name = Zip Code Handler
description = Provides a view handler to format a field
   as a zip code
package = D7 Views Recipes
; Handler
files[] = d7vrzch_handler_field_zip_code.inc
files[] = d7vrzch_views.inc

version = "7.x-1.0"
core = "7.x"
php = 5.2
```

3. Save the file as d7vrzch.info.

4. Create another text file and paste the following code into it:

```php
<?php
/**
 * Implements hook_views_data_alter()
 */
function d7vrzch_field_views_data_alter(&$data, $field) {
  if (array_key_exists('field_data_field_zip_code', $data)) {
    $data['field_data_field_zip_code']['field_zip_code']
      ['field']['handler'] = 'd7vrzch_handler_field_zip_code';
  }
}
```

5. Save the file as d7vrzch.views.inc.

6. Create another text file and paste the following into it:

```php
<?php
/**
 * Implements hook_views_api().
 */
function d7vrzch_views_api() {
  return array(
    'api' => 3,
    'path' => drupal_get_path('module', 'd7vrzch'), );
}
```

7. Save the file as d7vrzch.module.

How to do it...

1. Create another text file and paste the following into it:

```php
<?php
// $Id: $

/**
 * Field handler to format a zip code.
 *
 * @ingroup views_field_handlers
 */
class d7vrzch_handler_field_zip_code extends
  views_handler_field_field
{
  function option_definition() {
    $options = parent::option_definition();
```

```
    $options['display_zip_totals'] = array(
      'contains' => array(
        'display_zip_totals' => array('default' => FALSE),
      )
    );

    return $options;
}

/**
 * Provide a link to the page being visited.
 */
function options_form(&$form, &$form_state) {
  parent::options_form($form, $form_state);
  $form['display_zip_totals'] = array(
    '#title' => t('Display Zip total'),
    '#description' => t('Appends in parentheses the number of
                        nodes containing the same zip code'),
    '#type' => 'checkbox',
    '#default_value' => !empty($this->
        options['display_zip_totals']),
    );
}

function pre_render(&$values) {
  if (isset($this->view->build_info['summary']) ||
    empty($values))
  {
    return parent::pre_render($values);
  }
  static $entity_type_map;

  if (!empty($values)) {
    // Cache the entity type map for repeat usage.
    if (empty($entity_type_map)) {
      $entity_type_map = db_query('SELECT etid, type FROM
        {field_config_entity_type}')->fetchAllKeyed();
    }

    // Create an array mapping the Views values to their
        object types.
    $objects_by_type = array();

    foreach ($values as $key => $object) {
```

```
      // Derive the entity type. For some field types,
         etid might be empty.
      if (isset($object->{$this->aliases['etid']}) &&
       isset($entity_type_map[$object->{$this->
             aliases['etid']}]))
      {
        $entity_type = $entity_type_map[$object->{$this->
          aliases['etid']}];
        $entity_id = $object->{$this->field_alias};
        $objects_by_type[$entity_type][$key] = $entity_id;
      }
    }

  // Load the objects.
  foreach ($objects_by_type as $entity_type => $oids) {
    $objects = entity_load($entity_type, $oids);

    foreach ($oids as $key => $entity_id) {
      $values[$key]->_field_cache[$this->field_alias] = array(
        'entity_type' => $entity_type,
        'object' => $objects[$entity_id],
      );
    }
  }
 }
}

function render($values) {
  $value = $values->_field_cache[$this->field_alias]
    ['object']->{$this->definition['field_name']}
    ['und'][0]['safe_value'];
  $newvalue = $value;

  if (!empty($this->options['display_zip_totals'])) {
    $result = db_query("SELECT count(*) AS recs FROM
     {field_data_field_zip_code} WHERE field_zip_code_value =
     :zip",array(':zip' => $value));
    foreach ($result as $item) {
      $newvalue .= ' (' . $item->recs . ')';
    }
  }

  return $newvalue;
}
```

2. Save the file as `d7vrzch_handler_field_zip_code.inc`.

3. Navigate to `admin/build/modules` and enable the new module, which shows as the Zip Code Handler.

4. We will test the handler in a quick view. Navigate to `admin/build/views`.

5. Click on the **+ Add new view** link, enter **test** as the **View name**, check the box for description and enter **Zip code handler test**; clear the **Create a page** checkbox, and click on the **Continue & edit** button.

6. On the Views edit page, click on the **add** link in the **Filter Criteria** pane, check the box next to **Content: Type**, and click on the **Add and configure filter criteria** button.

7. In the **Content: Type** configuration box, select **Home** and click the **Apply** button.

8. Click on the **add** link next to **Fields**, check the box next to **Content: Zip code**, and click on the **Add and configure fields** button.

9. Check the box at the bottom of the **Content: Zip code** configuration box titled **Display Zip total** and click on the **Apply** button.

10. Click on the **Save** button and see the result of our custom handler in the Live preview:

```
field_zip_code:
229021234 (1)
field_zip_code:
20006 (2)
field_zip_code:
20006 (2)
```

How it works...

The Views field handler is simply a set of functions that provide support for populating and formatting a field for Views, much in the way a printer driver does for the operating system. We created a module in which our handler resides, and whenever that field is requested within a view, our handler will be invoked. We also added a display option to the configuration options for our field, which when selected, takes each zip code value to be displayed, determines how many nodes have the same zip code, and appends the parenthesized total to the output.

The three functions, two in the `views.inc` file and one in the module file, are very important. Their result is that our custom handler file will be used for `field_zip_code` instead of the default handler used for entity text fields. In the next recipe, we will add zip code formatting options to our custom handler.

Styling a view field

In the preceding recipe, we created a module for a custom field handler for a zip code and a small test view to see the result. In this recipe, we will add styling options to the handler to offer the user a choice of output styles.

Getting ready

This recipe continues from what was created in the _Handling a view field_ recipe. If you have not yet tried that recipe, please do, so that you will have the module and view necessary for this recipe.

Edit one of the home content types (or add a few if you have none). At least two of the nodes should have the same zip code, and at least one should have a nine-digit zip code without a hyphen, for example, 12345789.

How to do it...

Carry out the following steps:

1. Edit the file `d7vrzch_handler_field_zip_code.inc` and insert the following highlighted code in the `options_form()` function:

```
function options_form(&$form, &$form_state) {
  parent::options_form($form, $form_state);
  $form['display_zip_totals'] = array(
    '#title' => t('Display Zip total'),
    '#description' => t('Appends in parentheses the number
      of nodes containing the same zip code'),
    '#type' => 'checkbox',
    '#default_value' => !empty
      ($this->options['display_zip_totals']),
  );
  $form['type'] = array(
    '#type' => 'select',
    '#title' => t('Formatter'),
    '#options' => array(
        t('Zip+4 or Zip'),
        t('Zip'),
        t('Alphanumeric')
```

```
        ),
        '#default_value' => $this->options['type'],
    );
}
```

2. In the same file, just prior to the final }, insert the following code:

```
function _make_zip($value, $zip_type=2) {
  // remove the hyphen if present
  $zip = explode('-', $value);
  switch ($zip_type) {
    case 0: // zip+4 or zip depending on size
      if (is_numeric($zip[0])) {
        $value = $zip[0];
        if (sizeof($zip) > 1) {
          if (is_numeric($zip[1])) {
            $value .= '-' . $zip[1];
          }
        }
      }
      else {
        if (strlen($zip[0]) > 5) {
          $value = substr($zip[0],0,5);
          if (strlen($zip[0] == 9)) {
            $value .= '-' . substr($zip[0],5,4);
          }
        }
      }
      break;
    case 1: // zip (trim to 5)
      if (is_numeric($zip[0]) && strlen($zip[0] >= 5)) {
        $value = substr($zip[0],0,5);
      }
      break;
    case 2: // no format change
      break;
  }
  return $value;
}
```

3. Save the file.

4. Navigate to admin/structure/views and edit the test view.

5. Click on the link in the **Fields** box for **Fields: field_zip_code**, and at the bottom of the configuration box, select **Zip+4 or Zip** from **Formatter**, clear the **Display Zip total** checkbox, and click on the **Apply** button. This will provide a result as shown in the following screenshot:

```
field_zip_code:
22902-1234
field_zip_code:
20006
field_zip_code:
20006
```

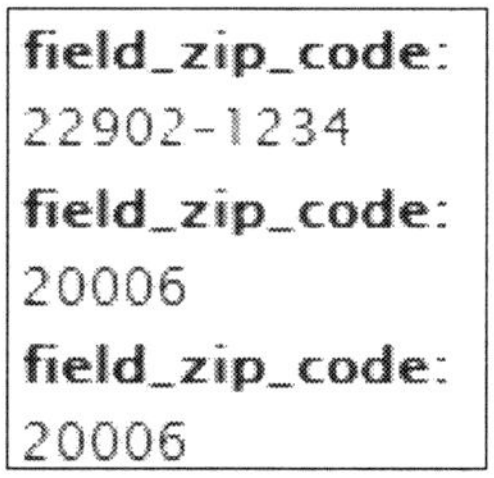

6. Click on the same field link once again, and this time select **Zip** from the **Formatter** and click on the **Apply** button, resulting in the output shown in the following screenshot:

```
field_zip_code:
22902
field_zip_code:
20006
field_zip_code:
20006
```

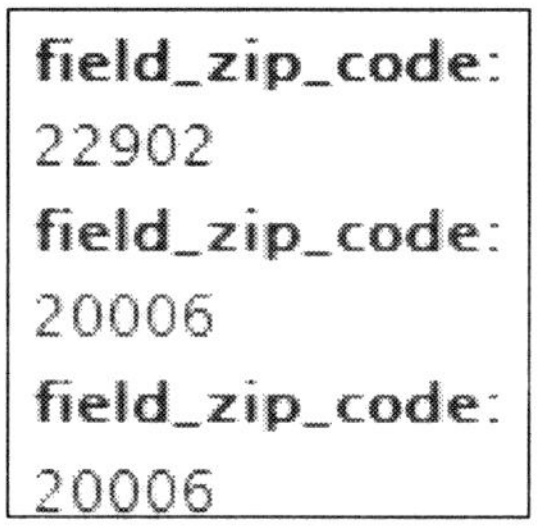

How it works...

The **Formatter** select box in the field configuration screen is merely a form field that passes along the selected value. The code we put in place created three options that are then fulfilled by a formatting function. The first option displays the zip code as either Zip+4 (12345-6789) or zip (12345), depending. If the zip code is numeric and either of the format xxxxxxxxx or of xxxxx-xxxx, it will be displayed as Zip+4, if 5 digits, as a regular zip code. The second option is to always display in a zip format, so that a longer zip code will be truncated to five digits. The third option leaves the zip code unformatted, which would be good for alphanumeric postcodes.

Fine tuning the query

The Views UI is a powerful query builder tool, in addition to its other functionalities, but sometimes the SQL query generated by it is not precisely what you want it to be. In this recipe, we will make a change to a view query.

Getting ready

This recipe continues from the test view and code created in the *Handling a view field* recipe. If you have not yet tried that recipe, please do, so that you will have the module and view necessary for this recipe.

How to do it...

Carry out the following steps:

1. Edit the module file `d7vrzch.module` and add the following code:

    ```
    /**
     * Implements hook_views_query_alter
     */
    function d7vrzch_views_query_alter(&$view, &$query) {
      if ($view->name == 'test') {
        $query->orderby[0]['field'] =
          'field_data_field_zip_code_node_entity_type';
        $query->orderby[0]['direction'] = 'ASC';
      }
    }
    ```

2. Save the file.
3. Edit the test view to see the preview, as shown in the following screenshot:

```
field_zip_code:
20006
field_zip_code:
20006
field_zip_code:
22902
```

How it works...

The underlying query in a view is made available as a data structure at various points in the view rendering process. We made use of a hook into the process and altered the query structure to change the sort field.

Why would you want to do this instead of simply using the Views UI? The Views UI is good for users to manipulate a view, given the applicable permissions, but those changes would be persisted until the view was changed again. In addition, you may want aspects of the underlying query to be handled dynamically, determined based on the data being queried, the user doing the query, or other factors.

7
Views Administration

In this chapter, we will cover some basic administration, including:

- Exporting a view
- Importing a view
- Bulk exporting views
- Cloning a view

Introduction

When working with multiple views and/or sites, it can become quite tedious creating every view from scratch. There are, however, ways to avoid this predicament. We will cover how to copy views, whether to another view or another site.

Exporting a view

Exporting a single view can be done very easily, but might not be something you have tried. Let's export one now. We will export a view that is installed with the Views module.

Getting ready

Navigate to the views list (`admin/structure/views`) and enable the `teasers_with_ backlinks` view if it is not already enabled.

How to do it...

Carry out the following steps:

1. Navigate to the **Views List** page (`admin/structure/views`).

2. Click on the down-arrow next to the **Edit** link for the **teasers_with_backlinks** view and click on the **Export** link, as shown in the following screenshot:

3. A textarea box populated with the php code required to recreate the view will appear. The first part of that code is shown in the following screenshot. Simply copy all the text from the textbox, paste it into a file, and save it. The filename and extension are of no importance; however, just be sure to remember what you name it and where you put it:

```
teasers_with_backlinks
$view = new view;
$view->name = 'teasers_with_backlinks';
$view->description = 'Displays a list of nodes that link to the node, using the search backlinks table.';
$view->tag = 'default';
$view->view_php = '';
$view->base_table = 'node';
$view->is_cacheable = FALSE;
$view->api_version = 3.0-alpha1;
$view->disabled = FALSE; /* Edit this to true to make a default view disabled initially */

/* Display: Defaults */
$handler = $view->new_display('default', 'Defaults', 'default');
```

How it works...

The export tool generates the code necessary to create the data structure that is created by the settings chosen for your view in the Views UI.

There's more...

If you are familiar with phpMyAdmin, the export will have looked familiar to you, as both tools function in a similar fashion. Similar to the SQL tool, the export is often followed by an import.

Importing a view

The tool to import a view will typically be used when moving from or to another site. When working within a site, the `Clone` function will typically be more useful. Still, importing is typically quick and painless. Let's try one.

Getting ready

We will be using the export code from the previous recipe, so take a minute and execute that recipe now if you have not yet done so.

How to do it...

Carry out the following steps:

1. Navigate to the **Views List** page (`admin/structure/views`).
2. Click on the **+ Import** link.
3. Under the import dialog that opens, provide a new name for the view. This will be a "machine name", meaning you should use lower-case letters, and underscore is the only punctuation allowed.

 Remember that the view's name appears in the export code. If you are importing into a site where a view with that name already exists, you must provide a new name to avoid a collision.

4. Paste the code to be imported into the **Paste view code here** textbox and click on the **Import** button as shown in the following screenshot:

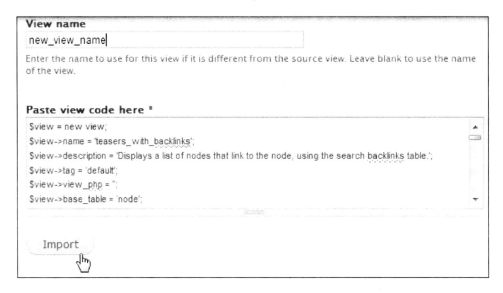

5. Now in the Views UI, remember to save your view!

How it works...

The `import` function takes the code that was exported and executes the php instructions, which are equivalent to having created a new view through the UI and manually selecting each of the view settings.

There's more...

Though simple, exporting and importing individual views is not the most efficient method when you have many in one site that need to be migrated. In that situation, it is much better to perform a bulk export, and that is the next recipe.

Bulk exporting views

One drawback of having views being stored in the database is that it makes it almost impossible to version the views. Keeping it in the code can overcome that, and also result in the code being executed more quickly. Not everyone is up to writing a view in the code though.

Moving views from one site to another can seem a problem, as the views are kept in several tables in the database. One can export each view, and then import it at the other site, but if you have many views, it can quickly become tedious. Being able to export several views at one time would be much better.

Views come with an **Exporter** module that resolves both of the preceding issues. It allows views created in the Views UI to be exported to a module.

Getting ready

The **Views Exporter** module needs to be enabled in order to use this recipe.

How to do it...

Carry out the following steps:

1. Navigate to the **Views List** page (`admin/structure/views`) and click on the **Bulk Export** tab, as shown in the following screenshot:

2. Select the views to be exported, as shown in the following screenshot:

VIEWS	TAG	DESCRIPTION
☐ blog_posts		Subsets of blog posts
☐ chameleon		Content type displays
☑ comments_recent	default	Contains a block and a page to list recent comments; the block will automatically link to the page, which displays the comment body as well as a link to the node.
☐ content_topics		Bulleted list of topics
☐ content_topics_facebook		Bulleted list of topics with Facebook buttons
☐ country_countdown		View title and Themed country rows
☐ course_list		A list of available courses
☐ custom_node_links		An index of site content, with each entry being a custom link
☐ department_course_list		Department information and available courses
☐ employee_extensions		Employee information and extensions
☑ frontpage	default	Emulates the default Drupal front page; you may set the default home page path to this view to make it your front page.
☐ glossary	default	A list of all content, by letter.

3. Scroll down past the end of the file list and enter a name for the module in which you will use the exported code, and then click on the **Export** button, as depicted in the following screenshot:

4. The Views Exporter module will give you three windows of code. The first you will save as my_module.info, the second as my_module.module, and the third as my_module.views.inc, replacing each occurrence of my_module with the name you provide for the module in step 4. The three files should be saved in a folder, typically with the same name as the module, and that folder should be located in the same directory used for custom modules on your site, probably sites/all/modules.

5. After saving the files, clear the cache (admin/config/development/performance).

6. Enable the new module, and your views will be found in the Views UI list.

How it works...

There are two files needed to create a module: the .info file, which describes the module, and the .module file, which contains the module code. The Views Exporter module creates these files, as well as the file that contains the code for creating a programmatic view. The reason you need to provide a module name is that this name is used in calls within the three files, and so needs to be known prior to code generation.

There's more...

You will notice that with your newly-modularized views, the choice of **Delete** has been removed from the views list in the admin panel and has been replaced with **Disable**. As the view is no longer in the database, it cannot be deleted, but it can be disabled, even though the module itself is enabled.

For whatever reason, there could be situations when you want the view to be residing in the database again instead of in a module. The easiest way to do this is to clone the view, which, once saved, will be a database-resident copy.

Cloning a view

Sometimes, you will need to create a view that is similar to another. There is no reason to create a new view and each setting within it systematically, when you can simply copy the original view and then make whatever changes you need.

How to do it...

Carry out the following steps:

1. Navigate to the **Views List** page (`admin/structure/views`).

2. Select the view that you wish to clone and click on its **clone** link (on the **Operations** drop-down)

3. The dialog that appears next is the same as when creating a view. Other than that, the view type cannot be changed; it must be the same as the original view. Choose a new name for the view, and change the description and/or tag(s) if you wish, and click on the **Next** button.

4. When the UI appears, be sure to save the view; it is not permanent until you do so.

Installing Views

In this chapter, we will cover the installation of Views.

In Drupal 7, the manner in which modules are installed has been greatly simplified. They can still be downloaded onto your computer and uploaded to your Drupal site as with Drupal 6, though the module package no longer needs to be decompressed, but the easier way is to simply provide the Drupal installer a URL for the module and let it do all the work.

Many people continue to have trouble getting the installer to function as designed, including me. If it seems to simply 'sit there' without downloading the module(s), switch to the manual method.

So, where do you obtain the URL? *You can obtain it from the* `Drupal.org` project site. Every contributed add-on module for Drupal has a project page. There, you will find a description about the module, links to its support page, download package, and sometimes, even documentation. These pages are found at `http://drupal.org/project/module_name`, where `module_name` is the desired module. Often, if there is more than one word in its title, the words will be connected by an underscore. In our case, we will navigate to `http://drupal.org/project/Views`.

You will often find that there is more than one version of the module available. You will want the URL of the download link for the **Recommended version** for the right Drupal release; 7.x for our use.

Take care when you use versions that have a suffix of `Alpha`, `Beta`, or `Dev`. `Alpha` means that the module is raw and is for community testing, and at this point, any of its features are subject to change. `Beta` is further along, and while the features are probably 'frozen', there can still be many bugs. `Dev` is a development snapshot, and can go from working to not working on any or all features from snapshot to snapshot. None of these is recommended for use in a production site. It is best to use a standard release, such as `7x-3.0`, without a suffix.

Installing Views

Carry out the following in order to install Views:

1. Navigate to the Views project page at `http://drupal.org/project/views` and scroll down to the **Downloads** section, as shown in the following screenshot:

Downloads

Recommended releases

Version	Downloads	Date	Links
7.x-3.0	tar.gz (1.39 MB) | zip (1.6 MB)	2011-Dec-18	Notes
6.x-2.16	tar.gz (1.21 MB) | zip (1.35 MB)	2011-Nov-14	Notes

Other releases

Version	Downloads	Date	Links
6.x-3.0	tar.gz (1.13 MB) | zip (1.31 MB)	2012-Jan-04	Notes

Development releases

Version	Downloads	Date	Links
7.x-3.x-dev	tar.gz (1.5 MB) | zip (1.71 MB)	2012-Jan-08	Notes
6.x-3.x-dev	tar.gz (1.13 MB) | zip (1.31 MB)	2012-Jan-08	Notes

Project Information

Maintenance status: Actively maintained
Development status: Under active development

Module categories: Content Display , Views

Reported installs: **364907** sites currently report using this module. View usage statistics.
Last modified: October 4, 2011

---

2. We can see that at this time, the recommended release of Views for Drupal 7.x is 7.x-3.0. We will install it. On a PC, right-click over the **Download** link beside that release and copy the link location. Choose the version you want, ZIP, or `tar.gz`. On a Mac, control-click over the link and choose the appropriate `Finder` command.

3. Navigate to the module's install page (`admin/modules/install`) and paste the URL you copied into the Install from a URL text box, and click on the **Install** button.

4. When the install has completed, click on the link to activate the new module. On the module page, scroll down to the Views module (probably at or near the bottom of the page) and check the boxes for **Views**, **Views exporter**, and **Views UI**, then click the **Save configuration** button.

5. If the installer does not work for you, download the package (ZIP or `tar.gz`) to your computer, decompress it, and use an FTP client to upload the resulting Views folder to the directory you are using for contributed modules, which is usually `sites/all/modules`.

6. Navigate to the modules admin page, `admin/modules`, and at a minimum, enable **Views** and **Views UI**.

B
Entity Types and Fields

This appendix discusses the details of the entity types and fields that are used in this book, and the instructions for creating them.

> The content types can be downloaded and imported by using the Bundle Copy module (instructions are included with the downloadable files). It can be downloaded from the code download link on the Packt site.

Creating content type: Country

This content type is used in the *Teaming two content* lists recipe in *Chapter 4, Creating Advanced Views*.

Details

The details of this content type are as follows:

- **Name**: Country
- **Comments**: None
- **Author information**: None
- **Field**: Area (field_country_area)
- **Type**: Integer
- **Format**: Text field

Creating content type: Country

Use the following steps in order to create the **Country** content type:

1. From the Admin structure menu (`admin/structure`) click on **Content types**.
2. Click on the **+Add content type** link.
3. Enter **Country** in the **Name** textbox.
4. Enter **Country information** in the **Description** textbox.
5. Click on **Display settings**.
6. Clear the **Display author and date information** checkbox.
7. Click on **Comment settings.**
8. Select **Hidden** from the **Default comment setting for new content** select box.
9. Click on the **Save and add fields** button.
10. Click on the **delete** link for the **Body** field and confirm the deletion.
11. Under the **Add new field** enter **Area** in the **Label** textbox.
12. Enter **country_area** in the **Field name** textbox.
13. Select **Text** from the **Type of data to store** select box.
14. Click on the **Save** button.
15. Click on the **Save field settings** button.
16. Click on the **Save settings** button.

Creating content type: Course

This content type is used in the *Understanding relationships* recipe in *Chapter 3, Intermediate Custom Views*.

 Create this content type after the Department content type

Details

The details of this content type are as follows:

- ▶ **Name**: Course
- ▶ **Comments**: None
- ▶ **Author information**: None
- ▶ **Field**: Course Number (field_course_number)

- ▸ **Type**: Text
- ▸ **Format**: Text field
- ▸ **Field**: Course credits (field_course_credits)
- ▸ **Type**: Integer
- ▸ **Min**: 1
- ▸ **Max**: 12
- ▸ **Field**: Department (field_department_ref)
- ▸ **Type**: Node reference
- ▸ **Format**: Checkboxes

Creating content type: Course

Carry out the following steps in order to create the **Course** content type:

1. From the **Admin structure** menu (admin/structure) click on **Content types**.
2. Click on the **+Add content type** link.
3. Enter **Course** in the **Name** textbox.
4. Enter **College course** in the **Description** textbox.
5. Click on **Display settings**.
6. Clear the **Display author and date information** checkbox.
7. Click on **Comment settings**.
8. Select **Hidden** from the **Default comment setting for new content** select box.
9. Click on the **Save and add fields** button.
10. Under the **Add new field** enter **Course number** in the **Label** textbox.
11. Enter **course_number** in the **Field name** textbox.
12. Select **Text** from the **Type of data to store** select box.
13. Click on the **Save** button.
14. Enter **36** as the **Maximum length**.
15. Click on the **Save field settings** button.
16. In the **Course settings** box, enter **12** in the **Size of text field** textbox.
17. Click on the **Save field settings** button.
18. Under **Add new field** enter **Course credits** in the **Label** textbox.
19. Enter **course_credits** in the **Field name** textbox.
20. Select **Integer** from the **Type of data to store** select box.

21. Click on the **Save** button.

22. Click on the **Save field settings** button.

23. In the **Course settings** box, enter **1** in the **Minimum** textbox.

24. Enter **12** in the **Maximum** textbox.

25. Click on the **Save** settings button.

26. Under **Add new field** enter **Department** in the **Label** textbox.

27. Enter **department_ref** into the **Field name** textbox.

28. Select **Node reference** from the **Type of data to store** select box. (Note that the CCK contributed module provides this field type).

29. Select **Checkboxes/radio** buttons from the **Widget** select box.

30. Click on the **Save** button.

31. Check the checkbox for **Department content type**.

32. Click on the **Save field settings** button.

33. Click on the **Save settings** button.

Creating content type: Department

This content type is used in the *Understanding relationships* recipe in *Chapter 3, Intermediate Custom Views*.

Details

The details of this content type are as follows:

- **Name**: Department
- **Comments**: None
- **Author information**: None
- **Field**: Chairman (field_department_chairman)
- **Type**: Text
- **Format**: Text field
- **Field**: Phone (field_department_phone)
- **Type**: Text
- **Format**: Text field
- **Field**: Degrees (field_department_degrees)
- **Type**: Long text
- **Format**: Text area

Creating content type: Department

Carry out the following steps in order to create the **Department** content type:

1. From the **Admin structure** menu (`admin/structure`) click on **Content types**.
2. Click on the **+Add content** type link.
3. Enter **Department** in the **Name** textbox.
4. Enter **College departments** in the **Description** textbox.
5. Enter **Department name** in the **Title field label** textbox.
6. Click on the **Display** settings.
7. Clear the **Display author and date information** checkbox.
8. Click on the **Comment settings**.
9. Select **Hidden** from the **Default comment setting for new content** select box.
10. Click on the **Save and add fields** button.
11. Under **Add new field** enter **Chairman** in the **Label** textbox.
12. Enter **department_chairman** in the **Field name** textbox.
13. Select **Text** from the **Type of data to store** select box.
14. Click on the **Save** button.
15. Click on the **Save field settings** button.
16. Click on the **Save settings** button.
17. Under **Add new field** enter **Phone** in the **Label** textbox.
18. Enter **department_phone** in the **Field name** textbox.
19. Select **Text** from the **Type of data to store** select box.
20. Click on the **Save** button.
21. Click on the **Save field settings** button.
22. Click on the **Save settings** button.
23. Under **Add new field** enter **Degrees** in the **Label** textbox.
24. Enter **department_degrees** in the **Field name** textbox.
25. Select **Long text** from the **Type of data to store** select box.
26. Click on the **Save** button.
27. Click on the **Save field settings** button.
28. Click on the **Save settings** button.
29. Click on the **Save** button.

Creating content type: Employee

This content type is used in the *Forming a dashboard with Page, Block and Attachment Displays* recipe in *Chapter 4, Creating Advanced Views*.

Details

The details of this content type are as follows:

- **Name**: Employee
- **Comments**: None
- **Author information**: None
- **Field**: Department (field_employee_dept)
- **Type**: Text
- **Format**: Text field
- **Field**: Position (field_employee_position)
- **Type**: Text
- **Format**: Text field
- **Field**: Employee ID (field_employee_id)
- **Type**: Text
- **Format**: Text field

Creating content type: Employee

Carry out the following steps in order to create the **Employee** content type:

1. From the **Admin structure** menu (`admin/structure`) click on **Content types**.
2. Click on the **+Add content type** link.
3. Enter **Employee** in the **Name** textbox.
4. Enter **Company employees** in the **Description** textbox.
5. Enter **Employee name** in the **Title field label** textbox.
6. Click on **Display settings**.
7. Clear the **Display author and date information** checkbox.
8. Click on **Comment settings**.
9. Select **Hidden** from the **Default comment setting for new content** select box.
10. Click on the **Save and add fields** button.
11. Under **Add new field** enter **Department** in the **Label** textbox.

12. Enter **employee_dept** in the **Field name** textbox.

13. Select **Text** from the **Type of data to store** select box.

14. Click on the **Save** button.

15. Click on the **Save field settings** button.

16. Click on the **Save settings** button.

17. Under **Add new field** enter **Position** in the **Label** textbox.

18. Enter **employee_position** in the **Field name** textbox.

19. Select **Text** from the **Type of data to store** select box.

20. Click on the **Save** button.

21. Click on the **Save field settings** button.

22. Click on the **Save settings** button.

23. Under **Add new field** enter **ID** in the **Label** textbox.

24. Enter **employee_id** in the **Field name** textbox.

25. Select **Text** from the **Type of data to store** select box.

26. Click on the **Save** button.

27. Click on the **Save field settings** button.

28. Click on the **Save settings** button.

29. Click on the **delete** link for the **Body** field and confirm the deletion.

30. Click on the **Save** button.

Creating content type: Extension

This content type is used in the Forming a dashboard with *Page, Block and Attachment Displays* recipe in *Chapter 4, Creating Advanced Views*.

Details

The details of this content type are as follows:

▸ **Name**: Extension

▸ **Comments**: None

▸ **Author information**: None

▸ **Field**: Employee ID (field_employee_id)

▸ **Type**: Text

▸ **Format**: Text area

Creating content type: Extension

Carry out the following steps in order to create the **Extension** content type:

1. From the **Admin structure** menu (admin/structure) click on **Content types**.
2. Click on the **+Add content type** link.
3. Enter **Extension** in the **Name** textbox.
4. Enter **Employee extensions** in the **Description** textbox.
5. Enter **Extension** in the **Title field label** textbox.
6. Click on **Display settings**.
7. Clear the **Display author and date information** checkbox.
8. Click on **Comment settings**.
9. Select **Hidden** from the **Default comment setting for new content** select box.
10. Click on the **Save and add fields** button.
11. Under **Add existing field** selection, select **field_employee_id** from the **Select an existing field** select box.
12. Enter **Employee ID** in the **Label** textbox.
13. Click on the **Save** button.
14. Click on the **Save field settings** button.
15. Click on the **Save settings** button.
16. Click on the **delete** link for the **Body** field and confirm the deletion.
17. Click on the **Save** button.

Creating image style: Exhibit

This content type is used in the *Changing the Frontpage view,* recipe in *Chapter 1, Modifying Default Views* and *Image styles* recipe in *Chapter 5, Intermediate Custom Theming Views*.

Details

The details of this content type are as follows:

- **Effect**: Scale and crop
- **Width**: 480px
- **Height**: 640px

Creating image style: Exhibit

Carry out the following steps in order to create the **Exhibit** content type:

1. From the admin Configuration page (`admin/config`) click on **Image styles**.
2. Click on **+Add style** link.
3. Enter **Exhibit** in the **Style name** textbox.
4. Click on the **Create new style** button.
5. Select **Scale and crop** in the **Effect** select box.
6. Click on the **Add** button.
7. Enter **480** in the **Width** textbox.
8. Enter 640 in the **Height** textbox.
9. Click on the **Add effect** button.
10. Click on the **Update style** button.

Creating image style: Exhibit_teaser

This content type is used in the *Changing the Front Page View,* recipe in *Chapter 1, Modifying Default Views* and *Image styles* recipe in *Chapter 5, Intermediate Custom Theming Views.*

Details

The details of this content type are as follows:

- **Effect**: Scale and crop
- **Width**: 120px
- **Height**: 160px

Creating image style: Exhibit_teaser

Carry out the following steps in order to create the **Exhibit_teaser** content type:

1. From the admin Configuration page (`admin/config`) click on **Image styles**.
2. Click on **+Add style** link.
3. Enter **exhibit_teaser** in the **Style name** textbox.
4. Click on the **Create new style** button.
5. Select **Scale and crop** in the **EFFECT** select box.
6. Click on the **Add** button.

7. Enter **120** in the **Width** textbox.

8. Enter **160** in the **Height** textbox.

9. Click on the **Add effect** button.

10. Click on the **Update style** button.

Creating image style: Exhibit_block

This content type is used in the *Changing the Frontpage view,* recipe in *Chapter 1, Modifying Default Views* and *Image styles* recipe in *Chapter 5, Intermediate Custom Theming Views.*

Details

The details of this content type are as follows:

- ► **Effect**: Scale and crop
- ► **Width**: 240px
- ► **Height**: 320px

Creating image style: Exhibit_block

Carry out the following steps in order to create the **Exhibit_block** content type:

1. From the admin Configuration page (admin/config) click on **Image styles**.

2. Click on **+Add style** link.

3. Enter **exhibit_block** in the **Style name** textbox.

4. Click on the **Create new style** button.

5. Select **Scale and crop** in the **EFFECT** select box.

6. Click on the **Add** button.

7. Enter **240** in the **Width** textbox.

8. Enter **320** in the **Height** textbox.

9. Click on the **Add effect** button.

10. Click on the **Update style** button.

Creating content type: Gallery

This content type is used in the *Changing the Frontpage view,* recipe in *Chapter 1, Modifying Default Views* and *Image styles* recipe in *Chapter 5, Intermediate Custom Theming Views.*

Details

The details of this content type are as follows:

- ▸ **Name**: Gallery
- ▸ **Comments**: None
- ▸ **Author information**: None
- ▸ **Field**: Image exhibit (field_image_exhibit)
- ▸ **Type**: Image
- ▸ **Format**: Image exhibit

Creating content type: Gallery

Carry out the following steps in order to create the **Gallery** content type:

1. From the **Admin structure** menu (`admin/structure`) click on **Content types**.
2. Click on the **+Add content type** link.
3. Enter **Gallery** in the **Name** textbox.
4. Enter **Gallery exhibits for use on the alternate front page** in the **Description** textbox.
5. Click on **Display settings** button.
6. Clear the **Display author and date information** checkbox.
7. Click on the **Comment settings** button.
8. Select **Hidden** from the **Default comment setting for new content** select box.
9. Click on the **Menu settings** button.
10. Clear the **Main menu** checkbox.
11. Click on the **Save and add fields** button.
12. Under **Add new field** enter **Exhibit image** in the **Label** textbox.
13. Enter **exhibit_image** in the **Field name** textbox.
14. Select **Image** from the **Type of data to store** select box.
15. Click on the **Save** button.
16. Click on the **Manage display** tab.
17. Select **<hidden>** from the **LABEL** (column) select box for the **Exhibit image field** (row).
18. Select **Image exhibit** from the **FORMAT** (column) select box for **Exhibit image** (row).
19. Click on the **CUSTOM DISPLAY SETTINGS** link.

20. Check the **Full content** checkbox.

21. Click on the **Teaser** tab.

22. Select **<hidden>** from the **LABEL** (column) select box for the **Exhibit image field** (row).

23. Select **Image exhibit** from the **FORMAT** (column) select box for **Exhibit image** (row).

24. Click on the **Save** button.

Creating content type: Home

This content type is used in the *Winning that argument in Chapter 2, Basic Custom Views, Nodes within nodes* recipe in *Chapter 3, Intermediate Custom Views,* and *Creating a view with multiple personalities* recipe in *Chapter 4, Creating Advanced Views.*

Details

The details of this content type are as follows:

▸ **Name**: Home

▸ **Comments**: None

▸ **Author information**: None

▸ **Field**: Zip code (field_zip_code)

▸ **Type**: Text

▸ **Format**: Text field

▸ **Field**: Image exhibit (field_image_exhibit)

▸ **Type**: Image

▸ **Format**: Image exhibit

Creating content type: Home

Carry out the following steps in order to create the **Home** content type:

1. From the **Admin structure** menu (admin/structure) click on **Content types**.

2. Click on the **+Add content type** link.

3. Enter **Home** in the **Name** textbox.

4. Enter **Homes for sale** in the **Description** textbox.

5. Enter **MLS ID** in the **Title field label** textbox.

6. Click on the **Display settings** button.

7. Clear the **Display author and date information** checkbox.

8. Click on the **Comment settings** button.

9. Select **Hidden** from the **Default comment setting for new content** select box.

10. Click on the **Menu settings** button.

11. Clear the **Main menu** checkbox

12. Click on the **Save and add fields** button.

13. Under **Add new field** enter **Zip code** in the **Label** textbox.

14. Enter **zip_code** in the **Field name** textbox.

15. Select **Text** from the **Type of data to store** select box.

16. Click on the **Save** button.

17. Enter **10** into the **Maximum length** textbox.

18. Click on the **Save field settings** button.

19. Click on the **Save field settings** button on the next screen.

20. Under **Add existing field** select **Image: field_image** from the **Field to share** select box.

21. Enter **Home image** in the **Label** textbox.

22. Drag the field and drop it below the **Zip code** field.

23. Click on the **Save** button.

24. Click on the **Save settings** button.

25. Under **Add existing field** select **Image: field_product_price** from the **Field to share** select box.

26. Enter **House price** in the **Label** textbox.

27. Drag the field and drop it below the **Home image** field.

28. Click on the **Save** button.

29. Click on the **Save settings** button.

30. Click on the **Manage display** tab.

31. Select **Inline** from the **LABEL** (column) select box for the **Zip code** field (row).

32. Select **<hidden>** from the **LABEL** (column) select box for the **Home image field** (row).

33. Select **Image medium** from the **FORMAT** (column) select box for **Home image** (row).

34. Select **<hidden>** from the **LABEL** (column) select box for the **House price field** (row).

35. Click on the **CUSTOM DISPLAY SETTINGS** link.

36. Check the **Full content** checkbox.

37. Click on the **Teaser** tab.

38. Select **Inline** from the **LABEL** (column) select box for the **Zip code field** (row).

39. Click on **Default** from the **FORMAT** select box.

40. Select **<hidden>** from the **LABEL** (column) select box for the **House price field** (row).

41. Click on **Default** from the **FORMAT** select box.

42. Select **<hidden>** from the **LABEL** (column) select box for the **Home image field** (row).

43. Select **Image medium** from the FORMAT (column) select box for Home image (row).

44. Click on the **Save** button.

Creating content type: Ingredient

This content type is used in the *Displaying a table of entity fields* recipe in *Chapter 3, Intermediate Custom Views*.

Details

The details of this content type are as follows:

 ▸ **Name**: Ingredient
 ▸ **Comments**: None
 ▸ **Author information**: None
 ▸ **Field**: Quantity (field_ingredient_quantity)
 ▸ **Type**: Decimal
 ▸ **Format**: Text field
 ▸ **Field**: Measure (field_ingredient_measure)
 ▸ **Type**: Text
 ▸ **Format**: Text field

Creating content type: Ingredient

Carry out the following steps in order to create the **Ingredient** content type:

1. From the **Admin structure** menu (admin/structure) click on **Content types**.

2. Click on the **+Add content type** link.

3. Enter **Ingredient** into the **Name** textbox.

4. Enter **Bulk ingredient for shopping list** in the **Description** textbox.

5. Click on the **Publishing Options**.

6. Enter **Name** in the **Title field label** textbox.

7. Click on **Display settings** button.

8. Clear the **Display author and date information** checkbox

9. Click on the **Comment settings** button.

10. Select **Hidden** from the **Default comment setting for new content** select box.

11. Click on the **Save and add fields** button.

12. Under the **Add new** field enter **Quantity** in the **Label** textbox.

13. Enter **ingredient_quantity** in the **Field name** textbox.

14. Select **Decimal** from the **Type of data** to store select box.

15. Select **Text field** from the **Form element to edit the data** select box.

16. Click on the **Save** button.

17. In **Quantity field settings**, click on the **Save settings** button.

18. Under the **Add new** field enter **Measure** in the **Label** textbox.

19. Enter **ingredient_measure** in the **Field name** textbox.

20. Select **Text** from the **Type of data to store** select box.

21. Select **Text field** from the **Form element to edit the data** select box.

22. Click on the **Save** button.

23. In the **Field settings** dialog box, click on the **Save** button.

24. In **Measure field settings**, click on the **Save** settings button.

25. Click on the **Save** button.

Creating content type: Product

This content type is used in the *Creating a Random Ad Block* recipe in *Chapter 2, Basic Custom Views* and *A Marketing Bundle* recipe in *Chapter 4, Creating Advanced Views*.

Details

The details of this content type are as follows:

- **Name**: Product
- **Comments**: None
- **Author information**: None
- **Field**: Product image (field_product_image)
- **Type**: Image
- **Format**: Image exhibit
- **Field**: Product price (field_product_price)
- **Type**: Decimal

Creating content type: Product

Carry out the following steps in order to create the **Product** content type:

1. From the **Admin structure** menu (admin/structure) click on **Content types**
2. Click on the **+Add content type** link.
3. Enter **Product** in the **Name** textbox.
4. Enter **Products for sale** in the **Description** textbox.
5. Click on **Display settings**.
6. Clear the **Display author and date information** checkbox.
7. Click on **Comment settings** button.
8. Select **Hidden** from the **Default comment setting for new content** select box.
9. Click on the **Save and add fields** button.
10. Under **Add new field** enter **Product image** in the **Label** textbox.
11. Enter **product_image** in the **Field name** textbox.
12. Select **Image** from the **Type of data to store** select box.
13. Click on the **Save** button.
14. Under **Add new field** enter **Product price** in the **Label** textbox.
15. Enter **product_price** in the **Field name** textbox.
16. Select **Decimal** from the **Type of data to store** select box.
17. Click on the **Save** button.
18. Click on the **Save settings** button.
19. Enter **$** in the **Prefix** field or any other currency symbol in the **Prefix or Suffix** field.
20. Click on the **Save settings** button.
21. Click on the **Manage display** tab.
22. Select **<hidden>** from the **LABEL** (column) select box for the **Product image field** (row).
23. Select **medium** from the **FORMAT** (column) select box for **Product image** (row).
24. Select **<hidden>** from the **LABEL** (column) select box for the **Product price field** (row).
25. Select **default** from the **FORMAT** (column) select box for **Product price** (row).
26. Click on the **CUSTOM DISPLAY SETTINGS** link.
27. Check the **Full content** checkbox.
28. Click on the **Teaser** tab.

29. Select **<hidden>** from the **LABEL** (column) select box for the **Product image field** (row).

30. Select **medium** from the **FORMAT** (column) select box for **Product image** (row).

31. Select **<hidden>** from the **LABEL** (column) select box for the **Product price field** (row).

32. Select **default** from the **FORMAT** (column) select box for **Product price** (row).

33. Rearrange the fields by dragging them so that order is **Product image**, **Product price**, and **Body**.

34. Click on the **Save** button.

Creating content type: Real Estate flier

This content type is used in the *Nodes within nodes* recipe in *Chapter 3, Intermediate Custom Views*.

Details

The details of this content type are as follows:

- **Name**: Real Estate flier
- **Comments**: None
- **Author information**: None
- **Field**: Property (field_home_nid)
- **Type**: Node reference
- **Format**: Select list

Creating content type: Real Estate flier

Carry out the following steps in order to create the **Real Estate flier** content type:

1. From the **Admin structure** menu (admin/structure) click on **Content types**.
2. Click on the **+Add content type** link.
3. Enter **Real Estate flier** in the **Name** textbox.
4. Enter **Body text and node references** for the **Week's hot properties** textbox.
5. Click on the **Display settings** button.
6. Clear the **Display author and date information** checkbox.
7. Click on the **Comment settings** button.
8. Select **Hidden** from the **Default comment setting for new content** select box.

9. Click on the **Save and add fields** button.

10. Under **Add new field** enter **Property** in the **Label** textbox.

11. Enter **home_nid** in the **Field name** textbox.

12. Select **Node reference** from the **Type of data to store** select box.

13. Choose **Select list** from the **Widget** select box.

14. Click on the **Save** button.

15. Check the box next to **Home**.

16. Click on the **Save field settings** button.

17. Select **Unlimited** in the **Number of values** select box.

18. Click on the **Save settings** button.

19. Click on the **Save** button.

Creating content type: Sponsor

This content type is used in the *Creating a Dynamic Links display block* and *Creating a Random Ad block* recipes in *Chapter 2, Basic Custom Views*.

Details

The details of this content type are as follows:

▶ **Name**: Sponsor

▶ **Comments**: None

▶ **Author information**: None

▶ **Field**: Sponsor logo (field_sponsor_logo)

▶ **Type**: Image

▶ **Format**: Thumbnail

Creating content type: Sponsor

Carry out the following steps in order to create the **Sponsor** content type:

1. From the **Admin structure** menu (admin/structure) click on **Content** types.

2. Click on the **+Add content type** link.

3. Enter **Sponsor** in the **Name** textbox.

4. Enter **Event sponsor** in the **Description** textbox.

5. Enter **Sponsor name** in the **Title** textbox.

6. Click on the **Display settings** button.

7. Clear the **Display author and date information** checkbox.

8. Click on the **Comment settings** button.

9. Select **Hidden** from the **Default comment setting for new content** select box.

10. Click on the **Menu settings** button.

11. Clear the **Main menu** checkbox.

12. Click on the **Save and add fields** button.

13. Under **Add new field** enter **Sponsor logo** in the **Label** textbox.

14. Enter **sponsor_logo** into the **Field name** textbox.

15. Select **Image** from the **Type of data to store** select box.

16. Click on the **Save** button.

17. Click on the **Manage display** tab.

18. Select **<hidden>** from the **LABEL** (column) select box for the **Sponsor logo** field (row).

19. Select **thumbnail** from the **FORMAT** (column) select box for **Sponsor logo** (row).

20. Select **<hidden>** from the **LABEL** (column) select box for the **Body** field (row).

21. Drag the **Sponsor logo** field above the **Body** field.

22. Click on the **Save** button.

23. Click on the **Full content** tab.

24. Select **<hidden>** from the **LABEL** (column) select box for the **Sponsor logo** field (row).

25. Select **thumbnail** from the **FORMAT** (column) select box for **Sponsor logo** (row).

26. Select **<hidden>** from the **LABEL** (column) select box for the **Body** field (row).

27. Drag the **Sponsor logo** field above the **Body** field.

28. Click on the **Save** button.

29. Click on the **Teaser** tab.

30. Select **<hidden>** from the **LABEL** (column) select box for the **Sponsor logo** field (row).

31. Select **thumbnail** from the **FORMAT** (column) select box for **Sponsor logo** (row).

32. Select **<hidden>** from the **LABEL** (column) select box for the **Body** field (row).

33. Drag the **Sponsor logo** field above the **Body** field.

34. Click on the **Save** button.

Creating taxonomy tags

This content type is used in the *Using related content: Adding depth to a term ID* recipe in *Chapter 4, Creating Advanced Views*.

Creating taxonomy tags

Carry out the following steps in order to create the **taxonomy tags** content type:

1. Navigate to `admin/structure/taxonomy/tags/add`, enter **Tourist Info** in the **Name** field, click on the **Relations** link, ensure that **<root>** is selected in the **Parent terms** list box, and click on the **Save** button.

2. Enter **Dining** in the **Name** field, click on the **Relations** link, select **Tourist Info** in the **Parent terms** list box, and click on the **Save** button.

3. Enter **Sightseeing** in the **Name** field, click the on **Relations** link, select **Tourist Info** in the **Parent terms** list box, and click on the **Save** button.

4. Enter **Lodging** in the **Name** field, click the on **Relations** link, select **Tourist Info** in the **Parent terms** list box, and click on the **Save** button.

5. Enter **Group Tours** in the **Name** field, click on the **Relations** link, select **Sightseeing** in the **Parent terms** list box, and click on the **Save** button.

Index

F

field
file_directory_path() function 105
template creating, steps 104, 105
theming 103
view creating, steps 103, 104
working 106
field handler, view 152-156
field_zip_code 156
file_directory_path() function 105
filter 69-71
Filter Criteria panel 28, 30, 32
filtering 81-84
Filters box 10
Filters section 75
food-topics page 83
Force single checkbox 24
formatter select box 159
Frontpage view
changing 14-16

G

gallery, content type
creating, steps 185, 186
details 185
glossary view
entries, selecting for specific user 17-20
grid
new view display creating, steps 108, 109
template creating, steps 109, 110
theming 108

H

Hide if empty checkbox 21
home, content type
creating, steps 186-188
details 186

I

ImageCache 136
image styles
about 136
attachment display creating, steps 138

block display, editing 137, 138
exhibit 182
Exhibit_block 184
Exhibit_teaser 183
page display, editing 137
views list 136
import button 166
import function 166
ingredient, content type
creating, steps 188, 189
details 188
Items per page textbox 127

L

Link this field to its term page checkbox 21
list-all-nodes 151

M

Manage fields tab 50
Management menu 40
marketing bundle 77-81
Master: Add filters 8, 10
Master display 18
Menu label textbox 38
module
creating 142-151
view, creating 142
monthly archive view
about 10
filter, adding 10
multiple content types
used, for creating bulleted list 46-48
multiple displays
course list attachment creating, steps 130,
131
department list attachment creating, steps
131
page display completion, steps 132
template creating, steps 133-135
theming 130
view list page, steps 130
working 135
multiple personalities
view, creating with 74-77

Thank you for buying
Drupal 7 Views Cookbook

About Packt Publishing

Packt, pronounced 'packed', published its first book "*Mastering phpMyAdmin for Effective MySQL Management*" in April 2004 and subsequently continued to specialize in publishing highly focused books on specific technologies and solutions.

Our books and publications share the experiences of your fellow IT professionals in adapting and customizing today's systems, applications, and frameworks. Our solution based books give you the knowledge and power to customize the software and technologies you're using to get the job done. Packt books are more specific and less general than the IT books you have seen in the past. Our unique business model allows us to bring you more focused information, giving you more of what you need to know, and less of what you don't.

Packt is a modern, yet unique publishing company, which focuses on producing quality, cutting-edge books for communities of developers, administrators, and newbies alike. For more information, please visit our website: www.packtpub.com.

About Packt Open Source

In 2010, Packt launched two new brands, Packt Open Source and Packt Enterprise, in order to continue its focus on specialization. This book is part of the Packt Open Source brand, home to books published on software built around Open Source licences, and offering information to anybody from advanced developers to budding web designers. The Open Source brand also runs Packt's Open Source Royalty Scheme, by which Packt gives a royalty to each Open Source project about whose software a book is sold.

Writing for Packt

We welcome all inquiries from people who are interested in authoring. Book proposals should be sent to author@packtpub.com. If your book idea is still at an early stage and you would like to discuss it first before writing a formal book proposal, contact us; one of our commissioning editors will get in touch with you.

We're not just looking for published authors; if you have strong technical skills but no writing experience, our experienced editors can help you develop a writing career, or simply get some additional reward for your expertise.

Ext JS 4 Web Application Development Cookbook

ISBN: 978-1-84951-686-0   Paperback: 450 pages

Over 130 easy to follow recipies backed up with real life examples, walking you through the basic Ext JS features to advanced application design using Sencha Ext JS

1. Learn how to build Rich Internet Applications with the latest version of the Ext JS framework in a cookbook style

2. From creating forms to theming your interface, you will learn the building blocks for developing the perfect web application

3. Easy to follow recipes step through practical and detailed examples which are all fully backed up with code, illustrations, and tips

Sencha Touch Mobile JavaScript Framework

ISBN: 978-1-84951-510-8   Paperback: 316 pages

Build web applications for Apple iOS and Google Android touchscreen devices with this first HTML5 mobile framework

1. Learn to develop web applications that look and feel native on Apple iOS and Google Android touchscreen devices using Sencha Touch through examples

2. Design resolution-independent and graphical representations like buttons, icons, and tabs of unparalleled flexibility

3. Add custom events like tap, double tap, swipe, tap and hold, pinch, and rotate

Please check **www.PacktPub.com** for information on our titles

PhoneGap Beginner's Guide

ISBN: 978-1-84951-536-8   Paperback: 328 pages

Build cross-platform mobile applications with the PhoneGap open source development framework

1. Learn how to use the PhoneGap mobile application framework

2. Develop cross-platform code for iOS, Android, BlackBerry, and more

3. Write robust and extensible JavaScript code

4. Master new HTML5 and CSS3 APIs

HTML5 Mobile Development Cookbook

ISBN: 978-1-84969-196-3   Paperback: 254 pages

Over 60 recipes for building fast, responsive HTML5 mobile websites for iPhone 5, Android, Windows Phone and Blackberry

1. Solve your cross platform development issues by implementing device and content adaptation recipes.

2. Maximum action, minimum theory allowing you to dive straight into HTML5 mobile web development.

3. Incorporate HTML5-rich media and geo-location into your mobile websites.

Please check **www.PacktPub.com** for information on our titles